SAUNTERING THROUGH APOCALYPSE

Serio-Comedy and Simple Spirituality

Jim Cleveland

authorHOUSE®

AuthorHouse™ LLC
1663 Liberty Drive
Bloomington, IN 47403
www.authorhouse.com
Phone: 1-800-839-8640

Published by AuthorHouse 04/04/2014

ISBN: 978-1-4969-0192-7 (sc)
ISBN: 978-1-4969-0195-8 (e)

Any people depicted in stock imagery provided by Thinkstock are models, and such images are being used for illustrative purposes only.
Certain stock imagery © Thinkstock.

This book is printed on acid-free paper.

by Jim Cleveland

SAUNTERING THROUGH APOCALYPSE

Serio-Comedy and Simple Spirituality

PART ONE
IN-sights, OUT-rages, and ID-iocies

by Jim Cleveland

PART TWO
Contemplations on Spirituality and Evolution

by Jim Cleveland

A Casual Introduction

In life, if you are able to develop a sense of humor and a philosophical attitude, you'll be all right. If they sometimes collide, it can get interesting.

I've found that a sense of the absurd is both funny and therapeutic, so I've written some stuff over the years that blunt the harsh realities of our societies, which are both greed-ridden and bloodthirsty. Rather than screaming at FOX and writing polemics about injustice, and instead of moaning about human foibles, there must be room to create things that induce laughter instead.

I will call it serio-comic. Maybe it's just satire. Maybe it's cathartic escapism. Maybe it's venom sweetened with corn syrup. It wound up on these pages anyway.

And then comes part 2 -- Massive content shift. A dichotomy to rock the publishing world's axioms? A polarity shift of nonsensical proportions?

These are personal explorations into Spirit anyway and they wound up on these pages too. For all the years that I have found humor to be an entertaining escape, and wrote these pieces, I was also exploring and writing on spiritual subjects, informed by the Urantia Papers, A Course in Miracles, the Pathwork and other new spirituality revelations that celebrate altrustic values.

All this co-exists here within a true Sense of Humor. Because a sense of humor is an integral part of our personality development. It isn't just laughing at jokes or skits or acts. A Sense of Humor is as much about a gentle smile, a caring and self-effacing attitude, a joyful knowledge of God, as it is about satirical belly laughs at our own infantile struggles. And spiritual growth and discovery is the prime source of joy on this world.

So here it all is together -- all related to Humor and also Good Humor.

What's it all about together? Is mining the planet Irony enough or is there a greater purpose?

Film Director Sydney Pollack once noted that before directing a picture, he had to study it at length and finally determine exactly what was the Spine of the picture. What was it about? For 'Out of Africa,' he summed it up as: Control.

I think this collection is about Values. -- Jim Cleveland

CHICKENS OF THE ROAD
Why did that chicken cross the road? As answered by...

National Organization for Women: Cross the road? Why? We should not be so oppressed that we HAVE to cross the road. The rooster should come to us. We are demanding equality and will not succumb to the lure of using seduction to get what we want. NOT!

Sierra Club: It is indeed a moot point for the road should not even be there. It created havoc for a whole population of grubs and worms, which should be preserved and safeguarded in their natural state for posterity. What will future generations of bears eat and where would we be without grizzly bears? Answer that one!

Carl Sagan: Speculation of a mere road obfuscates the critical need for the perception of a vast, cosmic reality, far above and beyond mere roads and into the far-flung galaxies of time, space and pretense.

Jim Bob Real: Cross the road? Don't let that chicken get away, Mama. Wring its neck 'cause the preacher is coming for Sunday dinner. And pour some oil gunk on the road. We got to settle that dust. It's cakin' up on them lovely pink flamingoes you just stuck up in the yard.

President Bush: That chicken has obviously skipped the coop and has nuclear weapons to hide. Get a wiretap on every barnyard worldwide. There could be oil under any one of them. If we can control all the barnyards in the world, we can corner the market on crude. Some say we've already done that but I think they're trying to be esoteric or something. Or maybe they're thinking of crud. That's different. That's like scum; it rises to the top.

Terrorist Izadore Goofus: Get road bombs out quick!! We blow up capitalist chicken and get supper at same time.

Terry Bradshaw: Lawdy Muzzy. I used to luv that fried chicken when I wuz a country boy. She's goin' out fer a pass, heah Fowl Feets, catch this ... and watch that transport truck! JJJezzzz and my goodness! It's as big as Mean Joe Greene wuz.

Foghorn Leghorn: I say, I say, now pay attention folks! That chicken is obviously under the spell of my bea-U-ti-ful I SAY Be-uti-ful red comb and I gotta say I got sumpin' for that Hot Mama. Come on over barnyard beauty and getta smack of this.

President of Mexico: No doubt, Chicken seek decent wages in Gringo Land, so we provide guidelines to assist in noble wetback flotation journey to yankee north, as chicken will no doubt take place in pecking order and wire much money home to family coop in our grand and glorious spongeball country.

by Jim Cleveland

Arizona Minutemen Volunteer Brigade **Capt. Billy Boob Tubbo:** "Git your guns on the line, boys, and keep a sharp eye out for alien chickens. They've already 'bout took up all the grit pickin' jobs in Texas."

Pluto (the dog): Better cross that road, and fast, chick-o cause I'm a' givin' chase. The media just said I wasn't real! Eating a live chicken should prove otherwise. Get Disney Studios over here. Or maybe Mel Gibson, and I can do it on camera!

James Bond: "First, I must meet the chicken and introduce myself. My name's Bond. James Bond. I will then decide whether to make love to her, shoot her or let the fowl beast pass. In the meantime, I'd like a martini, shaken not stirred. And an order of those hot chicken wings, please, with a bib.

Satan: I must sleep with this fowl first and then may she cross the road and spread her curse to all on the other side. Bring some Spanish fly and that apple wine.

Donald Trump: First, let's take a look at this chicken. Fat and ugly, right, like Rosie O'Donnell. Now, get outta here, no talent. Get across the road and out of the sight of anyone with talent and class, like me. I would never hire a chicken as an executive in my company anyway. They must be vicious and money-grubbing roosters. Like Rosie O'Donnell by the way.

Rosie: Look who's talking. I've seen better haircuts on orangutans. Thanks for the publicity. I'm inviting a number of chickens onto my show for a cacklefest.

Bill O'Reilly: It's clear to me, given the nature of this animal that she is a liberal and weak- spined do-gooder without the guts to cross that road and stay the course, as has our commander- in-chief, the President of the United States of America George W. Bush. I will pass on a response from the President's press office momentarily as they are in the adjoining suite.

Lou Dobbs: Clearly, such a crossing is a tragedy and an outrage. In the next hour, we will bring you a special report on the entire spectrum of illegal immigration and its powerful effects on the economy, the work force and the consumption of fried chicken in go boxes all along the American border.

Descartes: I think, therefore I am. I think that chickens do not think, but simply do. This is why they are merely part of the food supply.

Rachel Ray: Hey folks! No doubt this chicken was running to be part of a 30-Minute Meal! Today, we've got grilled chicken sausages wrapped in bacon clusters and slathered with a yummy yummy peppery tomato and minced capers sauce. What ya say? Yukko! Hey, guys, I understand. But this is my one thousand six hundred and ninety-first show and I've just time to change outfits before doing crabcakes and grit soufflé in the next segment down the hall. Hey! Get that chicken off the counter; she's pecking my corn meal.

Martha Stewart: I am sure she would want to cross to become part of an absolutely perfect dinner party, for which we are now going to create a stunning centerpiece made from corn flowers, a beautiful blend of white and gray chicken feathers and sprinklings of cracked corn. But first, these messages, and I need a few minutes to dump some stock.

Grandpa: In the old days, we always fed the chickens to keep them from crossing the road. When they got fat, we ate them. We didn't think about it. The chickens didn't think about it either.

Great Grandpa: Road? What's a road?

Great Great Grandpa: What chicken? Go shoot something with fur on it so we can eat and make a coat.

Chickens of the Road Literary Division:
Why Did That Chicken Cross the Road?

William Faulkner: Faced at the road, as he was and was all man with the eternal decision and quest of his existence and theirs concurrently, Lilliputian in both scope and feather-ness, beaked, extruding droppings, stenches of verbena, all the while and only to him alone because he alone knew it as it was, and only to him a supercilious symbol of myopic minimalism, smothered as it was by a nasty campus suicide and faded Faustian foistings of feigned agrarian glory that he remembered, mute as the sound and fury of idiots, torn from the Absalom artifices and orifices, castigated, castrated and calcified Snopesian landscape, a postage stamp of the chicken's banal barnyard reality, now gone with the wind of pedestri-an moonlight and roses cavalier prose, but to rise again, not only enduring and surviving, but somehow pretentiously, pre-ordinated, predetermined by destiny, the fowl fulminations that instigate an eternal evolutionary descent into banality and the opaqeness of reivers, as evidenced by a large yellow car at a whorehouse, and a return to mere soldier's pay with glories in between the intervening created sheets, filled with ink, therein, upon that ancient typewriter. Justly fortified, the chicken moved. She pulled on her purple robe and stepped resolutely across the barnyard to her shack, leaving the gravel road behind, as well as hot biscuits on the hearth for the gravy of mind, matter and the eternal circumstance of finding the road sacrosanct to all preconceived notions, quaint though Quentin once thought they were, stuffing his hands in his pockets strongly and plundering, stomping with incalci-fied guilt down the Yoknapatawpha dirt road, which had been the ripped and plundered hundred acres of his Sutphen souced soul, seemingly to him anyway in his thoughts of her, then him, them and theirs together as it had been, simply the rudimentarian ruminations within and upon this alley in which he peed, which rigorized his demand for Sartorian splendor, Compson compromise and the burping of hamlet homebodies, cretins amock in dusty, darkie courthouse intrusions, smouldering and bursting inside him, a saturation of sanctuary from a lost and prejudiced and putrefied region where Christmas was once called Joe, corn was compromised into an intrusive cob and Absalom ached with the artifices of ill-advised angst and aborted anticipations. And yet, by now, all chickens of the necessary parameters had been sacrificed upon the altar of Sunday Dinners, with an appalling floor full of Snopes chicks growing vociferously to replace them, crass over class. As I lie dying by the roadside, I hear the chicken pot simmering. I see a light in August. And yet it is but February on a broken watch, hearing a coffin being nailed together by illiterate hillbillies, and I forever live in an amber-colored and verbena-splashed past. I remain Nobel... and prized. The chicken remains undecided for the creature only has a blackeyed pea for a brain.

Shakespeare: To cross or not to cross, that is the question, and tis the only path to the Nunnery, where even now blank-eyed Ophelia strolls to the back garden with cracked corn and a wan, bird-like expression to feed such peckers as the forlorn chicken standing by the whizzing traffic. Alas, poor chicken, the interstate witches brew toil and trouble. Yon comes greedy Shylock driving a truck filled with a choking mass of chickens, soon to become broilers and fryers, beyond the knife, beyond the butchery of man. But in the end, we can only admit it's much ado about nothing. Shrews cannot be tamed. Fowl play cannot be abrogated. And eventually we must all cross the road. For Ophelia can't hurl that corn across that highway. It's four lane now. And the hunger within our bowels will always be filled with bowls of bitter brew before any higher consciousness we will be coming to. Hark, Rosen-kurds, I see an apparition now, a specter of this ungodly chow! Forsooth, it's f**king beans again. We must quit having lunch at the Nunnery! And <gasp> you say Romeo seasoned the beans!? Dreaded curse of the ages, the silly stylings of goofy young lovers, cursed and driven by impestuosity and hormonal whirlwinds, all scented with musk. Argh! I die now, and do my part in leaving the stage littered with corpses. As my vision fades, I see even now the glorious chicken dining in a green garden with my beloved Ophelia. We remain forever, in the words of Simon, crazy after all these years. I sleep, forsooth to have nightmares of blood and feathers on the highway. Death awaits us all unless we run like scared chickens.

Ernest Hemingway: They called him Chick. He stood there. He looked at the road. A moveable feast. The sun rises over it too. But this time, he had gone out too far. The bell tolls not for thee, but for my big tuna. Spoiled like tuna fish salad. Lost in the back of the refrigerator of life. Cold life itself. My life crumpled around me like a hit man's suit and the spoiled sandwich he carried in his pocket. Life's pockets are forever soiled as they are dark to the light. It is all bull, revealed my shit detector. Ole. I will kill the bull and fish. I will sail to the Keys. Eat Jerk Chicken at Sloppy Joe's. That is where it happened. Two strangers sat at the bar. Oh, shit, he thought. The detector had failed as had man himself. Herself too. He should have stayed at the road. By the Stop Sign. Now he said a silent farewell to arms. It was her arms he longed for now. He felt the last second with some remorse. The bullets ripped into him. The remorse grew. He was bleeding. The chicken was gone. He was left to die alone. He looked up at the barstool. It was raining too. The straw roof of life has holes. Butts had sat upon a stool he now could not reach with bloody fingers. The digits of the millions of touches in our lives. Had he been a soft touch? Or was he hard-boiled like an egg? He would lie wounded now without the answers, and look for a great mountain in his mind There must be snow upon it. It was life. It was all a snow job. He wanted it to be real, for once. He longed for the Chick he used to be, blasting elephants, hauling up fresh fish. His wounds were healing now. But the Cuban cook here would only bring beans. He knew only beans. Mankind only knows beans. Killing my joy ...Oh! And then two strangers walked into the room. They stood there. He had left his shit detector on the mountain. The cook stood there holding a steaming pot of beans. They shot him. He fell dead. I would have done so myself, he thought. In some other moment. In some other time. Then they turned to him. The gun felt cool to his grip. Then it went off. Theirs went off too. He wished he was back at Sloppy Joe's more than ever. Before all this started. He would have a beer and watch the chickens. They strolled freely over the island. They crossed roads. They crossed bridges. They were stupid and sometimes were killed. Like me. Now. At this moment. Today. The gunfight raged. Life goes on. Death too. I arouse myself and see a chicken make squat. It is on the floor. I take the beer bottle by its neck. I draw it back. I take aim. The chicken pecks something. I let it fly.

Dr. Seuss: Did this fowl go across this road? To lay a green egg, as I've been told? And why did this chicken go on the lam? To chase the cat that stole the ham? Hmmmmm?

Jean Paul Sartre: One must indeed ask why. A crossing would have no meaning, a symbolic gesture at best. She should sit instead and contemplate fate and the meaning of gravel and weeds by the side of that symbolically blacktopped thread. These are the roots of alienation. I pull up a little yellow flower and contemplate its fate that I have just produced of my own lethal free will. Will someone weed me in time? Other seeds are smothered under the black line. Shall I feel alienated because of it? Why the hell not? Since hell does not exist, but only its embodiments.

Charles Bukowski: The road is nothing. I will explore the Ditch in its deepest, darkest, stinkiest, most depraved form, great divisive gashes across the spectrum of everyday passages. I will have a bedroom scene featuring a large naked chicken and Charlie Sheen.

by Jim Cleveland

HEADLINES! Intergalactic Arts News Service:
Pioneering the Development of Robotic News for the Cosmos

DANTE'S INFERNO SCHMERNO
Author's Heirs-Sony plan sequel to Divine Comedy/Dante's Inferno.

As the 21st century unfolds, new authors will necessarily create lower depths in which to put deleteriously devolved evildoers. Telemarketing firms and spammers will both reportedly be included in lower echleon. Ann Coulter and the entire Fox news team are reportedly under consideration.

Authors refute possible Harry Potter tie in; don't rule out Flame-Grilled WhataBurger deal.

Authors may sue religionists for using characters and images from the first book to create a fallacious place which they use to scare the "hell" out of Christians; said to be basis of nefarious fear-based religion, now used widely to extort money, or "tithes," and make people pliant for use in military forces.

Film rights sold to Sony, which is rumored to be considering Godzilla as a central character interacting with the stars, Vin Diesel as Satan, Halle Berry as Princess Satan, and Angelina Jolie as a visiting journalist, who eventually adopts a fuscia-colored ogre and escapes to the Alps.

There was an effort to resurrect Stanley Kubrick from the dead to direct this picture, but the seance utterly failed, and left only a putrid stench in the room.

With Kubrick's unavailability, Sony is said be negotiating with the Farely Brothers but they seem insistent that crude bathroom humor be inserted. Hell's Bathroom would require the construction of a whole new set. Sony may yet turn to Martin Scorcese, who wants to shoot in New York City in August for the sake of realism, and make Satan a former Mafia Don.

Name of the picture is undecided. Cosmos Internet viewers may now enter titles. Here are some recently popular entries.

1 - Apocalypse Now II (Who knew? We thought it was Now ... Then.)
2 - Goin' Down With Dante (Black actor joins cast for rap theme song)
3 - Fry Hard! A terrorist band takes over Hades. Satan calls on Bruce Willis.
4 - Where Nightmares Wind Up (and where dreams never got to) with Robin Williams' evil twin added to cast)
5 - Inferno Schmerno Femme Macho! Jolie sheds reporter gear, stashes ogre in an empty tomb and does battle with old Horny Head with two laser pistols.
6 - Dante's Dreck. Dog named Toto 22 added to cast and pulls back curtain in hell's basement, exposes beatific posers who even want to make a buck out of God, or Hell, or Jesus, or Elvis or whomever. They are cursed with an eternity of watching Zig Ziglar tapes.

NEWS, THE GAME

They sit to have their faces made in little white bibs
They practice their pseudo reality in little bitty cribs
They hone the smile, clip the brows
And step out on the set.
Take their place on board facades.
No wise man has sat there yet.

They read the monitor that rolls the rote
Smiling through all the copy that's wrote
Thousands die and misery screams
But here's a commercial that whets your dreams.
It's all so awful, those wars and stuff
To balance it out, they'll toss some fluff.

They bring in hordes of pundits paid
To shill ideas in a passing parade.
They have no stallions of honor to mount
They're paid to swell their own bank accounts
Political ideas just management versus labor
The rich man's candidates or the working man's favor

They bask in bars and star struck cafes
They exult in the fame and their ratings forays
Their heads may be shallow but they have a fine glaze
That covers their beings like a lacquered malaise.
It's show biz, it's high rent, it's turning the screws
It's nothing any more than the evening news

They think about the depth that could add to the issues
They know their time is tight, though, thin like tissues
They varnish the surface and puff up the corporations
That pay all the way with advertising contributions
And so they point their exposes at other ones in their place
Who didn't buy the time and are now competitors to erase.

Here comes the news, a thing hard to define
It's slick and it's packaged like some bitter wine
It's calloused, it's cute. It waves many flags
Speculates and postulates as bigot guests brag
It zooms in on emotion and glorifies tears
It dotes on the grisly and plays up to fears
It's sometimes just confusing like some hanging chad
Often irrelevant like what the self-serving just said.
Here comes the news in its shallow streambed.

12

by Jim Cleveland

ADVERSARIAL ROLE

When I was back in journalism school,
They told me about this special rule:
You're an adversary, son,
And you don't trust the crooks.
They've riddled the government
They've cooked the books.
They lie to the people,
But you know the truth.
You're gonna expose 'em even
If you're uncouth.
Gotta stand up for the people
They gotta right to know
And you're the very reporter
Who'll cut through all the snow.
You know how to do it, son
Just stay in that adversarial role.
You're an adversary to corruption, son
Grab your pencil and go.

Well, I got some public relations work
for a big corporation.
Thought I'd be there for a long duration.
They said we gotta beat 'em boy,
And that's all the competition.
We'll run 'em out of business
And destroy their every ambition
It's the capitalistic way, son
Bankrupt 'em to drive attrition
You might even make the corporate royalty
Get in the Hilton penthouse position

That's where we kiss up to all the directors
And bribe them with every sweet
Soon you could be on the upside, fellow
Your money pouring out for treats.
Just make sure you compete like hell
Ring that cold hard business bell
For promotions, for your emotions
For your hot flashes and your colds
Just get on your suit and power tie
And play that adversarial role.

Well, my hair turned gray and I got to thinking,
What can I learn before I start sinking.
They told me to fight and always to win
Through this spinning adversarial life we're in. B
I'm thinking, and I'm blinking
It's them that's been kinking
Our life as it really should be.
Love One Another and not adversity.
I really don't think much of
Adversity.

Because I've heard lots of manipulating voices
Over the years demanding that I make their choi
And yet I don't see any good place they've left us
In fact, in a global mess is just where they've left
Gotta work together somehow to rise above dis-
honesty Which is driven by ...
You know it.
Adversity.

The Pupae of Irony

On the planet of Irony, somewhere in a galaxy like ours ...

One of the major religions there is the Cataract Church, said to be established originally by a saintly man who represented altruistic love, kindness, compassion, forgiveness, and a personal religion of feeding the hungry, clothing the needy, serving one another.

He was tortured and killed by two other collaborating religions, known as the Pagonads and The Juice.

The Cataracts reveled and worshipped in his martydom and said it was all the fault of all Ironians today, given the sinful aspect of breeding through the generations. One sin splattered all over everybody through the ages. They henceforth worked against the Pagonads and The Juice in every possible way. We're all guilty but they are worse because they actually did the deed.

Thank Goodness, the Saint had resurrected anyway, and some said: So what's the big deal? Mortal death is followed by resurrection. Let's try to work with the other religions since they really didn't know he was divine when they executed him for violating religious law and trashing the temple.

They were excommunicated, often tortured into a confession and then killed because of it.

Over the years the Cataracts changed to serve their inherent needs for power, wealth and control. This had irritated many, and the saintly man was now represented by other churches too. They thought they did do it better, and they thought the Cataracts were like eyesores, fighting many wars to prove it.

In the old days, the Cataracts had an army too, and some working deals with a number of others. Once a dissenting theologian named Marty published a critical editorial and they nailed Eddie to the church house door.

At one time deep into history, the 259th leader, or Pupae, of the Cataracts, FuddyDuddy III, died of senility and was revered as a Saint because he traveled broadly to do ceremonies. His frequent flier miles were astronomical, breaking the local galaxy record, which was set by Paris Hilton just before her symbolic crash into the Paris Hilton.

Under his regime, Cataract membership had plummeted by 30 percent and hundreds of priests had been convicted as child abusing perverts, draining the church's vast wealth in court settlements that had inexplicably been hoarded so that people could go hungry and needy and be beholden to them for a few showy alms.

by Jim Cleveland

It was a good strategy for a time but the pedophile scandal revealed a vast fortune, dubious financial dealings, and proved extremely costly during this Pupae's showy regime. He was named a Saint nonetheless, since the condition of the church was always the fault of its members anyway. And if the first Pupae could be a Saint, then why not everybody who held the office, except maybe Pope Pus IV, who genocided two races of people and burned down more than dozen libraries.

Seems that many ritualists on this planet had also gone over to the Pentecostarians who let worshippers be part of the church by feeling the holy spirit and singing and praising themselves instead of watching men march in robes and quote rote in monotone.

As people became well-educated, they left the Cataract church as being illogical and far behind the times, and interest waned. Why don't the adults get a choir already? And get these kids out of here and back home, where they will be safer.

FDII was named a Saint despite all of this, and even as many spiritual seekers of the age had discovered a personal relationship with God that made all else unnecessary. These dastardly Gnu Age people began to chastise the Cataracts for actually creating and promoting in the world Evil Curses. Those curses were named as:

Celibacy. A repudiation and dishonoring of one of God's greatest gifts to mortals, sexuality.

Sexuality. The church was charged with equating sexuality with evil and not celebrating it as a sacrament.

Child Abuse. A horror perpetuated by the sexual frustrations of celibacy and sex-guilt and associating it with evil temptation.

Gender Bias. Women had not been considered worthy of priesthood or wifehood. It was evident that the gender was as highly qualified as the other.

Birth Control. A massive worldwide need was short-circuited by the church's need to produce masses of little Cataracts.

Abortion. Made necessary by human stupidity and lack of church guidance, made so much worse by lack of birth control. Sperm does not have to be injected inside the female in sexual intimacy, Anti-Cataracts railed, plus medical science can prevent accidents, and adoption programs can manage them.

Abstinence. An idiotic concept promoted by the Church. Deprive yourself of God's gifts for awhile because you think he wants you to.

Sacrifice. Why would God ask for that? Silly concept designed to promote humility and subservience to really wise priests who kept all of the intellectual books away from the people to perpetuate their ignorance.

Guilt. People realized that they did not personally commit any sins at any time in history and are essentially responsible for their own lives today.

The Hell Myth. The church was accused of creating a mythical spiritual torture chamber to scare people into support.

Euthanasia. God doesn't ordain that people be kept marginally alive in a vegetative state. Critics asked: Where is the long-extolled Cataract faith? Why can't we make transitions without so much death fear?

Homosexuality. Truly commonplace through the centuries, but the church condemned it while providing it with a fertile environment. How could it possibly be a sin, many wondered. There is no credible evidence. A veil was lifted and the church fell into deeper disdain, revealed more as an arrogant, abstinence-poisoned despot, promoting sexual perversion and repudiation of God's gift of intimacy with one another.

Support of Horrible Regimes. The story was: Let the Cataracts come into the third world. We have big bribes for you, and then we will support your regime if you keep your crap under the table and help us build our missions. Indigeneous people are savages who must be conquered and civilized.

Finally, the church's history just became too much weight and it continued to decline as people began to feed their minds by actually reading and researching things as they were advised to do in the Stillness. The Pupae used to have armies, they discovered, and they slaughtered Pagonads all across Europe and desecrated their temples, women and children not excluded except for slavery.

Then, with all this condemning light coming in, and in desperation, the church's Redbird hierarchy counterattacked. All of these so-called evils charged against them were deemed to be devil-driven assaults against the Holy Church and its Eternal Values, by the Anti-Christ, no doubt. The reeling Cataracts appointed a tough-minded Pupae, GenoDick IV, who would take a renewed and strong stand for True Church Values against the onslaughts of thinking people, common sense and altruistic love of all people on of the planet.

But the more the new Pupae preached, he became increasingly irrelevant to people's minds and hearts and souls since postures were now known to be cheap and worthless in the light of realities. He railed on for a few years with a Return to Faith Inquisition to ward off the Anti- Christ. But new religions flourished, built upon a union of mind-body-spirit and a personal relationship with a cosmic First Source without regard to any silly dogma that some shysters would arrogantly deem Holy.

During this time, many of the people of Irony finally realized that the only possible thing that could be considered Holy in their world would not be a building or a location or a piece of history, or a document, or a church or a symbol or a folk tale or some guy's experience on the side of some road.

The only thing we are to make Holy is this world is our selves, our own personalities, they realized.

With this great knowledge, the people of Irony began working together cohesively and found an exciting adventure building the world to an era that they would call Light and Life. If we all love another, they thought, then it won't matter if all the religions and their tomes disappear. And so they began to actually disappear except for many which reformed for socializing, singing, potluck suppers and ice cream receptions and a lot of love among everybody, without any doctrine nailed to the door, or Marty either.

They studied and enjoyed many fine works of philosophy and science and theology and pure entertainment. Giant Worship Revelries filled stadiums and arenas and pastures worldwide. Thousands of voices rising up together in love.

The Inquisitor Pupae got more criticism than ever before. Membership continued to fall, and church members even more did what they pleased because it made spiritual sense to them in their personal relationship with God, and they didn't attend services much any more since they seemed to be senseless rituals compared to the exciting time they could spend at home with God, their loving Father, and Stillness sessions with friends. And they began withholding that 10 per cent tithe to more appropriately spend those dollars on direct needs of family and friends and refreshments to follow their meditation sessions.

Soon this Pupae passed on and the church Redbirds this time scrambled to find some way to save the church from its still growing irrelevancy and the continuing sex scandals, defections, lesbianism, fist fights breaking out in monasteries, protests by women dressed as priests and homosexual groups holding their own masses in the parks.

The next Pupae wanted to make amends and save the Cataract Vision. Clearly under pressure, the new exalted Pupae said that women could become priests. But by then women said they didn't want to be priests.

Priests can marry too. That's okay, came the general reply. We don't have to be a priest in order to marry. And Priesthood isn't nearly as much fun as my Stillness group and having my celestial teachers counsel me directly via the thoughts, questions and feelings in my mind.

Birth control in the name of God is okay too, said the new Pupae. Well, you don't have anything to do with it anyway, was the response. My relationships are my business, not some Pupae's, who doesn't even understand and experience the greatest thing on the human earth, family. He ain't been there or done that, so what does he really know?

We will sell much of the gold and real estate to feed more of the poor, said the new Pupae. He was simply asked why they hadn't done more over the centuries and why they had been so disrespectful and cruel to indigenous people.

So after all of this, and at last report, religious institutions were still coming and going and evolving on this planet of Irony, in this galaxy similar to ours. And the people there were coming and going and evolving too. The plan was working there too.

And as this evolvement led to opening up the universe circuits, people began to see all these similar, parallel adventures of evolving personalities on all these other time and space worlds in the various galaxies of the universe of universes. And people's minds and hearts were then really opened and they began to collectively say:

God Almighty! Look at all of these time and space worlds. Wow! And just think, we are all just children of the universe ... like little Pupae.

FEAR AND CONSEQUENCES

I got to worrying about the bird flu last week
and I took down the bird house.
I got to worrying about tornados
And them big oak trees that
could fall on my clapboard house.
So we pulled out the chain saws
And now I feel a little safer again
But I don't think I'll ever feel
Really safe on earth, my friend.
I'm generally afraid and it's mighty hot without some shade
And that really seems like an awful sin.

I got to worrying about the low lifes
I voted to take away all their support
And if they don't like the U.S. of A.
We got a massive prison business for their sort.
I pulled out all of the barbed wire
I could get out of my head
waved it all around me and made a muddy pen.
But when I saw all the hogs here,
It just seemed like a dirty sin.

I got to worrying about my faculties,
So I trusted the lawyers and the banks.
I felt uneducated to educate and so
The schools put my kids in ranks.
I got to worrying about God's punishments
Decided to walk the straight and narrow
Through pointed doors that smother spirit
And suck out your humanly marrow.
With religions fighting religions what a shape we're in.
And don't it feel like a faithless sin?

Where are you looking, my children and what do you fear?
Don't you know that God's plan is evolving right here?
If you falter in doubting when heathens are shouting
It's likely you'll not find the good cheer
To join the millions who Love you
And Love all Love below and above you
And know together we will rise above fear.
And the future belongs to no seer.
And it starts for us right here.

CHOICES OF SOUL

I left some blood on the iron
Left some sweat on the trail
Left some tears in the bedrooms
And bathrooms of hell.
I left some lovers in the doorway
Left some hate on the wire
Left some questions just hanging
About souls out for hire.

I watched myself leaving
Like I'd always done before
I watched in the mirror
Trying to keep up some score
Of the ravages and ridges
And contours of giving
Why am I not getting
More from this living?

Sweat came, then tears came and then came the blood
Remembrances, retributions and sliding banks of mud.
Time just keeps tearing; our facades are on fire
All twisted intentions of our souls here for hire.

I left regrets on some doorsteps
Left some hurt in my wake
Left some lessons unlearned
Clearly marked by mistakes.
Left some people with affection
Left some others in their ire
People buying and selling
All their souls are for hire.

I could sell my soul for wealth
Buy material, emotional things
Give it over to dogmas
That reflect our plastic dreams
Or I could keep it inside, safe
In God's eternal fire
Pledge my soul in faith
Make my soul free from hire.
I believe I can soar much higher

by Jim Cleveland

NEWS ITEM:
North American Interfaith Group Will Meet in Las Vegas

The continent's religious and spiritual leadership is being hosted by the U.S. in <gasp> Las Vegas

Sallying forth in their turbans and robes and beanies and rainbow togas, they will step out to be greeted by slot machines in every lobby, free poker chips at the hotel, and hookers wearing strings and spike heels accosting them on the strip. "Fellatio, Father?"

Unwholesome Holy Days in the Desert
Verse One: Great expectations for the city Bugsy built.

I'm leaving, Maria, for a Holy Place
A Shrine in the U.S. called Las Vegas
The world's great faiths will gather to see
the evils that scorch the family tree.
We'll see all that skin and beat down our urges,
disdain all those slots, avoid pocketbook purges.
Am sure there's an arena we can escape from the heat
with air-conditioned air all safe behind concrete.
and pray close-up here for those sinners outside
all stripped down and tanked up and acting so snide.
Come, Sinners, won't you come here and worship inside
All the world's faiths are here by your side.
We've got Sikhs and Jainists and Muslims and Jews
Protestants and Preterists and Preachers and Pews
Inside, we've got Baptists and Bahai's and Coptics
Catholics from Boston, Boise and the semi-tropics.
A world of religion here at your feet.
Every possible one, so please don't retreat.
But it's happy hour at Cito's, one wide-eyed guy replied
free hors' ovaries and them mozzarella sticks, fried.

Leaving Las Vegas, and Stubbornly Holy
Verse 2: Two cold showers were required

After a few days of duels in the Sodom
I am coming home, Maria, having seen the bottom.
Now renewed, we must fight this world's Gommorah
by not going there to meet no more'a
Next time there's a world interfaith camaradarie
We simply must go to Los Angeles.
City of Angels, a fine name. Can one suspect
how the glowing Sunset Strip must be so circumspect
with freedom, incense oils and the making of films
like X Men and X Men 2 and other such gems.
There's a heavenly mist over the LA blog
The residents, I think they call it Smog.
Ah, Maria, perhaps the Interfaith event
will lift this fog, make it California sunlit
and the Sunset Strip will see a Sunrise
And we will all become Holy
Wouldn't that be a surprise?

Urgently on the way home and pausing upon this
laptop and lusting for yours,
Eternally,

Ramon

by Jim Cleveland

PHANTASMAGORA

Pilgrims seek to grok and spiel
Understand what can't be real
Strike to burn the careless chill
Lick the blood from newfound kills
Stirring sparks that tempt the fates
Conversational souls relate
Shooting shit and venom peed
Spewing bits of serenity and screed
Holding wilted ties of flora
Hurts inside always told her
She could never escape
Phantasmagora.

Serious scholars came steeped in rote
Academy's sows and teeming shoats
Seek the robes and sashes and coats
Commencement airs, homecoming floats
Alumni give with every badge
That makes them love their very lives
Of precious giving and quarterbacks
Mazes of staunch academic tracks
The game in time became a mirror
With doubts of any better tomorrow
In semesters searching for
Phantasmagora

Wealthless struggle now takes the days
Nights of dread, purple haze
Working hard for Morgan and Chase
Boiling dry with the human race.
Beaten by banks and mortgage ruse
Lost in greed-drifted subterfuge
Indignities that we must choose
Institutions in mental recluse.
Hamsters turn the wheels of power
Times to brave, times to cower
At times I held back the horror
Lay back with TV's
Phantasmagora

Passion pricks the cold, dark skin
Surging surrogates, lifted chins
Truth that swells and bursts within
Alienating our closest kin
Searching on in fields of stumps
Languid boulders, beaten chumps
Hard to lift and move such rumps
Ripping grass in browning clumps
Bin Laden gone from Bora Bora
Years roll on to spread the horror
Read the news
Phantasmagora

I like the name but what could it mean?
Strikes me like a darkling queen
Phantasmagora,
I'm sure I've seen her on the screen
Phantasmagora
Sensations wrapped in passing scenes.
Phantasmagora
Such a word for reality's dream
Phantasmagora

The Perfection of Imperfection Plan

Scene: *A place called Havona, the upper realm of the Heavens near Father God's residence on the Isle of Paradise. All of Havona was astir. The Father had never conceived such a plan as this.*

Astarina glided through the wave back home, where she embraced her beloved Astar with a scintillating vibration, swirling with him in ecstasy, and then anxious to tell the news she had heard at the central ampitheatre.

The concepts are so profoundly different, she exulted. First of all, we have been denoted as being in what is called Perfection. It is the status that we have always experienced.

And there are other concepts, previously unrevealed? asked Astar. He had just returned from an exploratory adventure on a garden sphere and had not heard this first broadcast.

Yes, she said. While in the state of perfection, all is well and in the Father's universe plan. But now the Father will create imperfect creatures, those who might example those very traits of destructiveness that we have heard about recently in theory.

Astar responded. But why would He do such a thing? To create that which represents error and is not in perfection seems to pervert the great wisdom that He teaches.

We are told, she said, that it will be for our learning and experience, so that we may truly understand the lessons that we have been taught. Perhaps it will also be an extension of our experience.

And yet, said Astar. I don't know that I would ever choose to experience evil. Perhaps I understand it well enough.

In truth, said Astarina. This adventure is not for our primary experience but rather for our monitoring. The First Source proposes to send a legion of workers out into the vastness to create worlds of what they will call Time and Space. As I understand, it means that this Time has a beginning and an end, the state of finiteness of which we have already had theoretical preparation.

Yes, said Astar, I now see the value in some of these lessons. And Space, I suppose, is also a contained reality. The two concepts work together to compartmentalize. Then will the Father fill these creaions with new beings who are im-perfect? But why? Surely there is more reason than for our education and entertainment.

This is the amazing part, said Astarina. They will be evolutionary from the bare essentials of matter. Over time, these spherical gardens of botanical and animal life, such as on Zooania, will evolve to support advanced life that is capable of realizing the Father's existence, then on and on through a great expanse of evolution to actually, in the end, become One in perfection with God. Amazing is an understatement.

Astar asked: But how can animal or botanical matter become Godlike. It boggles the imagination!

She explained: The First Source will, Himself, create a special order of beings which will, at a certain time, be implanted in each of these evolving animals and they will eventually be transformed -- even though this must be accomplished through succeeding generations since there is a finite amount of time for each of them. They grow to a primacy, but then these organisms wither, sicken and die. I don't know why. What knowledge they have gained they must learn to pass on. There is also accidental death, for there will be much danger in these spheres.

No doubt from the volatile interactions that might occur, Astar surmised. Will these special beings of the Father that indwell these material ones have the power to control them for Truth, Beauty and Goodness?

Not really. As I understand it, the evolvers will have free will, and will only listen to the Father if they choose and succeed in making the connection

Brilliant, mused Astar. A vast laboratory-not just for us, but for the new beings. They are challenged to disdain their basic natures for divine ones through an internal monitoring system. And yet they can't actually attain it because their lives are finite. They couldn't possibly live that long, could they, in bodies made of matter. They must work together-multi-generationally.

That's not all, my lover, said Astarina. Of course, they can't make it in the first exercise, but the Father is creating a whole machinery of teaching facilities to resurrect these material beings and bring them on to perfection through an elaborate ascension plan. It's all going to be outlined during the coming Source-I broadcasts. They have an unlearned but growing mortal existence, and then they learn from it in the ensuring universe schools. This all sounds more elaborate and vast than even all of Havona.

And how will we be able to serve this mission?

By greeting these finite-to-infinite beings as they succeed in reaching us here, she responded. We will bring them the final distance to perfection.

Astar was thoughtful. You know, this is the most incredibly complex and thought provoking enterprise that we could imagine. The Father continues to amaze me with his spectacular creative concepts and skills.

And think of this, my soul mate, said Astarina. There will eventually be trillions of these beings in billions of worlds, coming on-line all the time during evolution, and all unique, and each personality on each world will also be uniquely different from any other, yet all from one divine pattern.

Once this project is begun, she went on, worlds will be created constantly and this will become an eternal reality itself. Establishing spiritual life within the basest of unknowing creations of matter and bringing them to Havana Perfection. There will be many types of these beings, all initially antagonistic toward one another. They must learn to love one another, know and love God, and build civilizations from these worlds that are composed only of raw materials.

They will surely need a lot of help.

Yes, at a given stage, the First Source will send a Planetary Prince, then later a Material Son and Daughter. I tell you, this plan is unbelievably elaborate. It is fascinating even to behold this first basic outline of a plan that will apparently continue forever.

Astar said: We are so blessed that the Father would give us participation in such a miraculous event. But the material beings ….will they all be brought upward? Or will there be failures? Those who will die and just be gone? It seems such a daunting task, rather impossible in the first generations. Yet, I can't imagine the Father ever failing at anything.

Yes, mused Astarina. But if He chooses to create imperfection, failures may be part of the plan. He might well create with the idea that only some will succeed. That's a concept we haven't experienced either.

Yet it would seem that what the Father would create, He would want to bring to fruition. For it seems quite certain that the Father would not propagate the illusionary concept of evil of which we have heard. It would seem that He would create beings who are truly capable of overcoming error and evil. Yes, by being endowed with these internal adjusting spirits. I am confident that the system will indeed work and we'll be welcoming these pilgrims to Havona in the fullness of the plan.

I wonder how they will look. Will they be anything like us? Astar wondered. Are we part of the pattern too?

Well, said Astarina, we are told that the patterns will remain inviolate, that there are a great number of variations that will be activated from the patterns that we already have.

But why imperfection? Why will the Father make his work unfinished? Is it that He would have the creatures gain cognizance and finish their development themselves? In that sense, is it a co- creative process between God and these material beings?

Yes. Yes! That vibrates me. What a concept! There are so many variations within this magnif-icent and yet unfathomable plan. Create a basis and then let the creatures develop them-selves. And to give them guidance, implant them with a monitoring spirit from the Father himself. So the Father gets to experience it all too.

Each generation of these beings will do its part, individually and collectively, to bring these worlds to perfection, even as departing ones follow an educational plan that will lead them here. And eventually, all will come to a Oneness with the First Source, as we are.

How exciting, said Astarina. I will love meeting and embracing new beings who are so different from ourselves.

What an adventure it will be, said Astar. We had best start getting ready for the first arrivals.

Escape from Sedona

SCENE: *The Hollywood offices of Globus, Gorbus, and Goofus Productions. A pitch is being made. Puffy Seams, a sweaty and amply-bellied promoter stands and twirls like Dumbo, with wide eyes and sweeping gestures. Behind a Mahogany airport of a desk, J.B. sits stolid, puffing methodically upon a huge cigar. His beady eyes squint, seeking vainly to find a crevice whereupon to make a dollar, a vision to complement Puffy's usual overwrought rhetoric, engulfed, as usual, in his own smoke ... and that of others.*

Puffy speaks. "I tell ya J.B., it's a natural. A third sequel in a series just getting settled in, like Jason and Freddie. They've had Escape from New York, I mean, who wouldn't? Ha! Uh-h. Snake Pleskin gets established there. Then Escape from L.A., with the newest pyrotechnics and minimalist script techniques. And now -- the Snake looms again!"

Puffy's fat fingers spun and waved upward, not like the dancing cobra he would emulated, but more like link sausages ascending to Heaven.

"This new adventure takes us to the mysterious New Age epicenter -- EzzzzCape from Sedona! Eerie red rocks, dead spirits floating, doing deep echoes, lots of dry ice, shadows, sharp objects. We do a gory murder before the credits to set the stage, gag some old farts walking their poodle or something. And then, in the midst of this mystical mayhem comes Snake Pleskin. Vacationing with a buxom girlfriend, a blonde since she needs to get captured later by dark-skinned devil cultists.

"Yeah? Which girl is that? I got some contracts from the day bed I gotta do sumpin' on," said J.B.

"Well, you know, somebody who looks good naked. She'll have to get tied up and laid out on a stone slab at some point," Puffy reasoned. "But anyway, Kurt and the girl get sucked into a netherworld ..."

"Wait a sec," J.B. grunted. "Gimme a minute to consider this load so far. I'm shakin' out my boots heah." This was always the cue for Puffy to shut up and give rapt attention.

Puffy looked like Thomas Gomez on a bad day. On a good day, he could do no better than Dane Clark. He listened, lips and brow pursed as if anticipating great wisdom, in truth anticipating something truly repugnant. He waited before the gnomish semi-mogul.

J.B. had reared back and looked upward, fingers joined, cagelike, puffing and watching his wafting, twisted ringlets. Like smoke off a manure pile, groused Puffy silently

J.B. finally shifted his squeaking recliner and dusted the cigar ceremoniously. "In the first place, Puffy, new age ain't shit for a market. Too much God business. They ain't gonna come see this pix. They're goin' for angels and elevator music. And our base adolescent market.

28

You'll drive them away in droves. They don't know Sedona from Baloney. And they don't know Yahweh from Maui Wowie! So let's blow this one off and keep givin' 'em what they want, decadence and the F-word screamed loud and frequently. Hardcore revenge. A golden calf. That's where the money is. How about … Tijuana?"

Puffy was deflated, mind buzzing with alternative arguments or ways to kiss J.B.'s ass and soften his view.

"Great idea!" Puffy spun. "That's how we can make it real. A Pagan Idol Snake Cult from Mexico. Snake Pleskin! What a tie-in! You're uncanny J.B. We were gonna use Colombian drug dealers or a devil cult but they've been done to death."

"Sure as hell have," J.B. enthused. His genius was taking hold. "But we gotta stay in the muscle and action category. Can't go into horror. It'll cannibalize our Chainsaw Bimbos series and the Children of the Corn. By the way, where are we on that one? The Corn Kids doing the devil shit."

"Puked out at 13," said Puffy, "the one where Morgan Fairchild and Godzilla, transported through time, came to the cornfields to confront Karo, the giant corn syrup blob. I'm sure you remember spending all that money engulfing Cedar Rapids? And the day somebody put the syrup in Morgan's shampoo!"

"Sure," said J.B., "and we got sued by the chinks over that rubber lizard. Godzilla, jeez, how can you copyright a name like that? It's kinda sacrilegious."

Puffy recalled that Rubbermaid of Japan, which had bought the rights, had sued them and won over the Godzilla image. Putting a pencil-thin mustache on the behemoth had been clever but ineffective with the court.

"That was a great series, J.B.,"Puffy kiss-assed, "but it was really time to put it in the crib - Ha! corn crib, get it? - uhh-h. Anyway, especially after making only $75 on the last one, and, of course, after the attempted suicide of the head scriptwriter and the damages to the cafeteria awning and everything … it kind of soured the scene, but! All the more reason we need to … Escape to Sedona." Puffy rallied.

"Wide screen this one, J.B. Evil new agers made into zombies, running amok. Helpless flower children get squashed by big red rocks that come alive. It's the dark side to all this spiritual whoo-whoo stuff. You know, them Angel books flying out of the stores. But all that means is that the bottom third of the taste test market, the one we've carefully cultivated with cool explosions, property damage, vengeance, vulgarity and fornication, is going to need our pictures more than ever as kind of an … antidote to all that warm honey running from the top of the market, the Yech! market. So, ironically, we tap good vibes to fuel bad vibes. For every action, a reaction; for every good idea a bad one…for every mature thought an adolescent pimple of a micro-thought that proves, nonetheless … profitable!"

"It can't miss," Puffy enthused. "And make it now, before them yellow perils over at Sony sign up Kurt for Escape from Tokyo or Yokahama or some other Pacific Pooh-Pooh. Let's pitch some good 'ol American escapism here."

"Hey, give it a rest, Puffy," J.B. grunted sourly. I gotta think here." Puffy wiped sweat from his brow and reached for the water pitcher.

"Of course! " boomed J.B. momentarily, as if he had just accepted the reins of planetary government. "Rocks! .... that come alive! That's new. Isn't it?"

"Why .... hell yes!" Puffy agreed in a loud, whispering rasp, as if he had just discovered the secret of life and the lottery. "An incredible insight, J.B. Live boulders, real big nasty ones! They'll come at you,with .... levitation! You know. The guys up in Santa Barbara are good at that. They can float in and ..... socko! He banged his fat fist. And rockslides, we'll have a big one at the end, with all kinds of noise and miniatures."

"Yeah," rasped J.B., "and then the real story underneath, in a cave we'll have a lost tribe of Amazon women. They wear string bikinis and shoot laser pistols. That'll give us some explosions and stuff to threaten Snake with."

"String bikinis?" blurted Puffy. "I was thinking about a bunch of big ugly hairy underground shits. You've got all those costumes left over from "The Monkey Shining."

"Babes in Bikinis!" J.B. insisted. "I've got to deal with those couch contracts. Marlene's been out of town. Besides Kurt can't kiss hairy things. Except on his own time. But we can use the hairies too, in supporting roles. That'll help Accounting get their dollars out of that buy. And work in that pit of animated vipers I paid big bucks for, remember, for the Hydra in Hot Pants deal."

"It's gonna be great, J.B. A blockbuster. But remember, when we start doing those rock squeezes, we can't get over three barrels of blood on official requisition or they'll put us out of Action and into the Horror category. Plus ...Action's the genre Kurt's looking for, unless Goldie talks him into one of those feel-good crappers she's always doing. Too bad she don't come around to our thinking. She'd look damned good lying naked on a slab."

"Kurt'll snap at it," Puffy went on. "You gonna use Dennis Hopper for the mad villain again, huh? He always has good weed."

"Why not? He's still the best whacko for the money," asserted J.B., "but remember that clause where he always gets to write his own dying scene, as it says his 'wry and comical last words.'

"Yeah, I thought that last one, where he drank kerosene and killed the canary with his final breath was a bit much. I don't think it symbolized the fate of mankind, like he said. It was just ... so much halitosis."

"Better to have halitosis than no breath at all," mumbled J.B. "I just want to see the statement beforehand. It better be funny, or he's never going to die on my screen again."

In subsequent weeks, Kurt and Goldie were approached about a third sequel in the "Escape From" action series. Kurt appeared aloof, but in time a sum of money was mentioned to Globus, Gorbus and Goofus that sent J.B. into a tantrum. He railed loudly of greed, dictating a letter to certain of the stockholders while puffing voraciously into the smoke-laden room.

And there, down the hall, waited the Japanese.

Sony made the third picture in the trilogy and it hit theaters in time for Christmas business. "Escape from Mars" featured the continued exploits of Snake Pleskin, scruffy antihero with a patch over one eye and a demonstrated and oft-used efficiency with a wide variety of firearms.

Mars has been turned into yet another penal colony where every scumbag of the universe has again been incarcerated. Snake is again heroic in that kind of sardonic, cute, cynical way and he eventually rescues the Venusian nurse hostages with the push-up bras from a fate worse than exposure.

The seeming millions of miscreants which Snake is called upon to dispatch in three barrels or less are made even more evil because they have been enslaved on this miserable space rock for nearly a millennium, in a kind of horrific tupperware party that goes on forever. It is hosted by Joan Rivers, and is punctuated with frequent intermissions in which the prisoners are forced to eat tiny finger sandwiches on rye bread and drink an exceedingly pale herb tea.

Once unleashed by an unthinking janitor, the galactic cretins take vicious bloodletting revenge to new depths of dementia. Hapless victims are thrown into pits of molten tupperware, which bubbles vulgarly while claiming its ludicrously screaming and rapidly-descending bodies -- a kind of modern-day version of the Pagan firepit.

Kurt, of course, once sufficiently irritated by atrocities and loaded with quips, wreaks havoc upon evil each day, working up a good appetite for meeting Goldie and friends for dinner.

They never did do "Escape from Sedona," and into the 21st century they were making features centered in Hong Kong, Peking, Sumatra, and even Berlin, in a timedrop where Kurt single- handedly wipes out a division of Nazi storm troopers. In a clever plot twist, the prisoners were the good guys this time, American fliers shot down by scantily clad alien Nazi women and a mob of big, ugly hairy things.

Today, Puffy has retired to Sedona. Though he still enjoys stuffing his face, there seems just a touch of sadness about him for the Big Picture he never made. Despite his enormous wealth and girth, he is often moodily reflective.

At moonlight he walks a tiny Chihuahua on a bike path under the enormous red rocks and often imagines that massive crimson bulk coming alive to burp guturally and smother joggers, meditators and backseat lovebirds alike in its horrific, beyond-granite grip. It doesn't happen.

Now, in hindsight, he realizes their mistake. They were off-base from the beginning. There's no doubt that Sedona should have been established, from the outset, as an intergalactic penal colony.

Puffy stands and waits patiently for Gomez, the Chihuahua, to leave a cigar-like turd at the base of the big red rock.

by Jim Cleveland

Newsletter:
This Week's New Titles at Out There Bookz

Down and Out with Beverly Sills. The opera star's college roommate with a touching memoir about their days as starving co-eds.

Gone With the Wendt. Actor George Wendt's best-seller about shedding 99 pounds on a diet of salted peanuts and light beer.

A Streetcar Named Bizarre. Sequel to the classic play, now a melodrama, with Blanche Dubois as a mysterious witch with heavy make-up who sells potions in the French Quarter, and Stanley returning home scarred from his life as a New York dockworker and sometime boxer.

Cocky. (a novel) A novice Hispanic boxer and day laboring gigolo who worships Rocky wants his fighting rooster to earn him the entry fee for the Oakland Golden Gloves.

Take the Money and Sun. A guide to the coolest and hottest vacation spots in the Caribbean. Billion Dollar Maybes. Investor Sly Stealman shares his secrets on speculating in the market.

Love With (the) Proper Strangler. (photography) Stylist Suzanne Cilantronella allows photographers to record her unrivaled collection of jeweled chokers. (With 69 color plates)

Love with (a) Proper Strangler. (novel) Heroine is romanced and set up to die by serial killer who only uses ultra-expensive neckties.

Love with this Proper Wrangler. Gay romance hits the rodeo circuit and cowpunchers go balls to the walls to protect their heterosexual tradition in this Tom Robbins bestseller.

Chicken Run. A collection of news essays on the final days of the Bush White House. A Man Called Coarse. Unauthorized biography of pornographer Larry Flynt and his courageous drive to win a medal in the Special Olympics.

Munster's Balls. How a determined band of entrepreneurs succeeded with an unlikely show about monsters settling into bickering family bliss and ushered in a new era of goofy monster caricatures on television.

Man of A Thousand Feces. Biography of the late New York City sewerage department commissioner Rush Brown, whose courageous actions saved the city from a methane gas explosion which would have sent tons of raw sewage and up to 100,000 sewer rats into the city streets. Soon to be a major motion picture with Tommy Lee Jones and Dennis Hopper.

Cool Hand Puke. A concise guide to the art of vomiting safety following an alcoholic binge, and appearing to still be cool to the girls while doing it. A bestseller on college campuses.

Pot on a Catty Tin Roof. Tennessee Williams' long lost memoir about weed-smoking and gay camaraderie on the roof of the French Quarter YMCA.

Oh, Brother, Where Art Their Art? A museum collector's guide to the actual geographical locations of numerous pieces of immortal and immoral art.

From Beer to Fraternity (novel). Young fraternity pledge wants to give up brawling and binging after a tragic accident, but fraternity officers put the pressure on to show up at Butthead's Beer Bust. Meantime, the Sigma Chis are rumored to be attacking the fraternity's house with a rain of water balloons.

The Purpose-Given Life. Mia Furst's bestselling spoof of the bestseller extols how richness itself provides purpose in life, and everything else, such as hard work, is cow pooey.

Lust for Leif. Pieces of an ancient manuscript allegedly written by explorer Leif Erickson's lover, who lived in ancient Norway. X -rated for descriptive scenes of fulfilled lust and graphic cruelty, murder and dismemberment of nordic animals and a crude, detailed description of how to turn them into stew. Signed by "Olga" this publishing sensation is a combination homemaking guide for an ancient age, and affectionate, melancholy lament for a wandering husband.

Get Thee Behind Me, Satin! An industry insider's passionate polemic to boycott satin sales, which allegedly provides funding for terrorists, and save the endangered cotton and polyester markets it threatens.

The Man Whose Gnu Tooted Too Much. (mystery) Inspector Waverly cracks a ring of smugglers using gnu stomachs to store and transport drugs. Flatulence intelligence holds the key to solving a series of across-the-border criminally-generated stampedes that carry the drugs to the coast, but also into the inspector's clever ambush.

The Bourne Silliness. Bourne seeks to unmask a mystery killer from his past as both rehearse for a Gilbert and Sullivan operetta. Bourne with an uzi, in a tutu!

Long Jay's Turning into Night. (novel, horror) Millionaire playboy Jay Bloodworth is gradually turning into a vampire werewolf who drinks too much. His Cuban mistress, Conchita, likes it, but his wife, Agnes, is aghast and calls the pound.

Days of Fine End Poses. (novel) An idealistic corporate couple fall into despair when their idealisms are shattered, slipping into an endless 24-7 addictive rut between Starbuck's and Ed's Comer Bar.

The Fandom of the Oprah. An analysis of the growing popularity of Oprah Winfrey by a team of race sociologists from Slippery Rock.

by Jim Cleveland

To Heal A Mockingbird (novel, sequel) Career woman Scout returns to Alabama hometown to help Mayor Boo Radley infiltrate the KKK and renovate his house. Soon a major motion picture with Robert Duvall and Holly Hunter.

King Dong. Biography of the late porn star and fabled I I-incher Biff Johnson, who died suddenly after accidentally ingesting 40-day old bong water.

Humpback Ravine (sequel) Broken-hearted gay cowboy finds romance again managing a highway rest stop, where appears handsome groundskeeper Riff Rock, holding a symbolic rake and scratching seductively.

Full Metal Iraq Hit. Unpublished, unfinished manuscript from the late Stanley Kubrick, updating his earlier film about Vietnam, and moving the scene to Iraq. In the harrowing first part, police force inductees in Baghdad endure 8 weeks of rigid training and are all blown up on a bus. In part two, an embattled patrol of GI's is ambushed by a one-eyed street beggar and forced to kill a friendly puppy carrying an explosive. The volume includes a collection of highly expressive rejection letters from film studios and a photograph of two yards of piled cow manure allegedly delivered to Stanley's carport by Sony Pictures.

Heart of Apocalypse Darkness. Protagonist and former assassin kayaks deep into Cambodian jungles to find a crazed hippie photographer and his commune of sex worshippers and get photos for Playboy. He decides to kill him and take his place. Soon a major motion picture with Charlie Sheen, Dennis Hopper, and Tio Tequila.

A Beautiful Hind. Mentally challenged genius professor lapses into panic when confronted with coeds in tight skirts. With professional help, he whips booty fixation and constructs a Nobel prize-winning formula to help scientists learn to better understand the nature of equations. Soon a major motion picture with Russell Crowe, Robin Williams, and Angelina Jolie as The Killer Equater.

Two Thousand and Juan: A Space Ecstasy. An Hispanic sweet potato field worker escapes a dying planet in drag disguise and finds himself on a spaceship with 2,000 refugee women from a Spanish fly factory.

Charlie and the Caribbean Chocolat Factory. Revolution in Haiti threatens a madam's chocolate banana stand until she is whisked away by a gypsy pirate with bad teeth and financed with a factory of her own in Tortuga before an evil missionary priest throws beach sand into her batter and violence ensues.

BOMBSHELLS OF THE CREATIVE MIND

SCENE ONE: *offices of MovieMagic.com in Oxnard, CA, one of the premier Internet multi-media sites for broadcasting, downloading movies and marketing related products.*

Characters: Rollie Allgood: *a 30-something staff member and Internet radio personality*
Chip Fritz: *Internet radio host and shipping clerk, a 20 something.*
Sergio: *near 20 intern supported by the International Media Institute, Naples, Italy.*
Midge Dewy: *broadcasting assistant and substitute host for the Internet radio station.*
Dietrich: *a punk intern.*

The time is near noon in a simple back office forged into a storage room at Movie Magic. Sergio, a small statured and studious young man is in his late teens, with pale white skin, wearing a shiny gray suit and open white shirt with a loosened narrow purple tie. He sits at his small desk under a pale lamp and on the telephone. He has a pencil-thin mustache.

Sergio: But Ma-ma, I understand that the harvest season is near, but I know that Carmelo will see to it. It will get done. I am just too busy here in the USA. I am working for one of the internet's largest and most prestigious presenters of film, global film. We have an amazing library and our own radio station, on the Internet.

Mama: *(appears at stage left, on the telephone)* How do I know of such things. I say, okay, you go to school. You go to school. A flem school, you say. Okay. I say, okay, but now they send you to a place called Oxnard. A home for oxen? I don't understand. And the only nets I know should hold fish.

Sergio: Ma-ma, I am learning the business. The movie industry liked my essays and were very impressed that I have seen so many of their films. And so they let me work here like an ... apprentice. But. I am called an in-tern. I have explained this. And I am making ninety-five dollars every week..

Mama: I am not making money here, my son. We are low of potatoes and fuel oil ...

Sergio: *(hearing noise of approaching people)*: I will send money. I promise. Love, love, love, love, goodbye, Ma-ma.

Mama: *(looks at the dead receiver)* I call for money. I get ... lovelovelove. This will not buy fresh potatoes. (hangs up the receiver in disgust and walks away.)

Sergio: *(watches anxiously as Rollie and Chip come through, pulling on their coats.)* Sirs .. sirs, excuse me. I notice you walk through here for lunch time ...

Rollie: *(spins around, still moving)* Yes, my good man. I hope we haven't disturbed the sanctity of your ... office here *(looking disdainly at the nearly bare desk)* Apologies all around. *(sweeps his arm to include Chip).*

Chip: Yeah, me too. We're just out to grab a bit of lunch. Who the hell are you, anyway, brother. I seen you about but ain't spoke.

Sergio: Intern. I am from Naples ... Italy. I am a writer. And I am here to learn everything about the business of movies. I learn, I work. I serve. *(smiles broadly)*

Rollie: Yeah, I heard about that at staff meeting. And ... you serve right here, huh? Like doing what?

Sergio: Processing media packets, press packets. We have one for just about everything. If we don't, I go to the Internet and make one.

Chip: Man, you got all the whole company by the balls. And right here!

Rollie: Well, I'm just down with the new stuff as a rule. You can hump the archives. But maybe you can help me with an idea I've been having.

Sergio: I would be so pleased. And, as a matter of fact ... I was hoping to speak with you about actually ... ummm ... Doing some writing, some real writing. I ... file very well and can work the Google, but ... I 'm a writer, a writer. I am.

Chip: Do what your heart commands. My heart-burn is calling for the Gorilla Burger.

Rollie: My idea is a definitive piece of work, Sergio. I've got my latest notes right here *(pulling a note pad from his day calendar, ripping off two pages and thrusting them at Sergio).* I gotta go, but here. These are comparative lists. Okay. The greatest bombshells of all time. The very biggest box office and critical successes. And this one ... the biggest bombs of all time, the absolute busts, lost a ton of money, critics ravaged them. Are you following me?

Sergio: *(takes the notes and looks at each of them)* Big hits ... Big busts ...

Rollie: I'm off, Sergio. Just got an hour. But write me up a short review of the top ten for each list. And these are just ideas, some no-brainers, see? But you pick 'em. In fact, the evidence is right there *(gestures to file cabinets).* You've got it all. I'll plan to get a draft from you in a few days. And, hey, 25 words max on each one. Title of the piece could be ... Bombs and bombshells: What's on your lists? You see, Sergio, it's all in the mind and the eye of the beholder. What is good or bad .. great or slimy ... silly or profound. And box office is not always the good measure ... nor the critics. Losers make money; winners sometimes don't. It's a dichotomy. Or an irony? Not sure which. Are we connecting here?

Sergio: I will present this to you tomorrow. I am anxious to begin my new career.

Rollie: Tomorrow? Well … all righty then. Maybe we'll buzz through here about lunchtime. But if you don't have time …

Sergio: No, no. I mean … yes, yes. I have time. I sell time. I am a new capitalist and I seek to impress. Ha! I am a poet and do not know it. Though … I suppose I do. Have a happy lunch.

Chip: Go get 'em Serbio. *(mocking The Terminator)* We'll Be Back! *(closes the door behind them)*

Sergio: *(holds the lists and turns them this way and that)* Bombs …bombshells … busts … Dolly Parton? … Bursting … By the rocket's red glare … *(he rubs his head worriedly, but then looks up resolutely, with strong resolve.)* I have read every press packet in the world. I have seen hundreds of films. It is time for Sergio … To surge! In 25 words or less. These narratives must be … crown jewels in my career … my new career as a … writer! *(he holds the two papers and purses his brow and lips, turning them this way and that as the scene darkens.)*

SCENE TWO: *(Midge walks into the recording studio at Movie Magic's 24/7 Internet radio station. Chip is on the air.)*

Chip: *(as the music ends):* All right then, that's the theme from Instant Eros and we've been talking with the composer and director by telephone from Paris, France, Mr. Peter Quatro, about music scoring in the virtual age. Join us next week for another guest on Virtual Virtuosity. And now, after a short movie news break, stay tuned for Rollie's Follies, chatter and caterwaul about movies today. This is Chip Fritz, signing off until tomorrow. *(turns a switch and puts down headphones)*

Midge: Hi, Chip. Sorry I'm late.

Chip: You've got to go on. You ready? Rollie came down with food poisoning. I told him to stay away from the oysters.

Midge: Me? But … I haven't done this show.

Chip: Rollie's got a canned show. It's on the top of his desk, on the right, well, I dunno. Maybe on the left. Just rip it and read it.

Midge: *(looking worried)* Well, I can read it. I can do that, sure.

Chip: Well, duh, you may have to do some ad lib around it. Welcome to radio *(leaves)*.

(A haggard Sergio walks into the studio, yawning and holding some paper-clipped pages.)

Chip: Sergio, what the hell?

Sergio: I've been up all night. Mr. Allgood. *(holds up papers)*

Chip: Put them on his desk. Midge, you'd better get busy.

(Sergio and Midge scramble to get to Rollie's office while Chip puts on his coat and begins to leave. They bump into each other going through the door, with both apologizing. The cubicle is cramped.)

Sergio: Excuse me. So very sorry. Please, this is for .. Mr. Allgood *(hands her his papers).*

(Midge rolls her eyes, takes the papers and smiles at Sergio sardonically as he leaves. She puts them on the desk and begins scrambling through the other papers there, soon creating a mishmash while hurriedly checking the dwindling time. Finally, in frustration, she leaves the desk in a mess and runs to catch Chip. Too late. She comes back and furiously shuffles through them again.)

Midge: Oh crap, where is it? Where is it? *(finally pulls out a neatly-typed paper.)* This must be it. *(looks through the other papers again and looks back)* Hell, yes, this has to be it. *(pulls on the headphones and checks the time, hurriedly reading through the text.)*

(Scene darkens; light comes up at stage far left to show Rollie Allgood at home, suffering in his pajamas and bathrobe, sitting haggardly at the computer with a burp pan close by, making the connection to his show. The broadcast begins.)

Midge: Good afternoon movie fans. Sad to say, your usual host Rollie Allgood is a little under the weather today and this is Midge Dewey sitting in. But never fear, the show is right here. As you know Rollie is probably the most knowledgeable expert on movies on the Internet and he's left us a pretty great show today. Let's roll forthwith, where's the drum roll anyway? First, the good news. Rollie's own personal and certainly well-informed picks for the top ten movie bombshells of all time, with a short and colorful synopsis of each. And here they are, Rollie's hit parade of the finest quality cinema of the ages ... a top ten of greatness.

Number 10. Heaven's Gate. Classic American tragedy told in epic style by Michael Cimino. Breathtaking visuals resemble classic art. Provocative irony permeates a startling denouement and unforgettable climax, which dissects the question of who rescues who in our lives, if at all.

(Rollie stands up from his computer, aghast.)

9. Howard the Duck. George Lucas' masterwork, an amazing juxtaposition of barnyard humor and intergalactic travel, with the incredible dry wit of our most unforgettable feathered personality. Move over Donald, Huey, Dewey and Louie too.

(Rollie swoons and falls over unconscious on the floor.)

8. The Postman. Kevin Costner's poignant vision of a post-apocalyptic world centered around postal delivery and the eternal struggle against evil.

7. Shanghai Surprise. The magic pairing of Sean Penn and Madonna and her ironic nun turn proves a casting masterstroke in an adventure that deftly blends laughs and larceny.

6. Gigli. Ben Affleck and Jennifer Lopez strike charismatic gold and screen sparks in this insider's tale of fame, fortune, fickleness and fortuitousness, and with a modicum of tongue-in- check profundity.

5. Ishtar. Dustin Hoffman and Warren Beatty, masters of drama, ham it up in an offbeat Crosby- Hope like road adventure. The flatulent camel is an historic Hollywood don't miss!

4. Water World. Costner the Master, at it again with an epic tale of a mutant fish-man and a mad bomber, conflictingly consummating a microcosmic phantasmagoria of aqua good-evil conflict that mirrors our struggles even on dry land.

3. Return to Oz. The old tale grows up in a sobering drama of the realities of time and mankind's penchant to destroy, even a magic kingdom. A powerful social document of what could happen to us!

2. Reefer Madness. Serio-comic satirical classic that uses childishly bad performances to underscore the eternal tight-assed ignorance of the human species.

And now ..... number one. Plan 9 From Outer Space. A visionary classic that expands the mind to myriads of possibilities from the nonsensical to the unexplained. Brilliantly realized minimalist scope on a small budget that provided a blueprint for hundreds of bare-budget exploitations to come.

(Rollie comes into consciousness on the floor and groggily manages to stand up and fall into the computer chair).

Midge: Okay *(laughs uproariously)* We're on a roll. Let's check out Rollie's other list. This one is Rollie's 10 Biggest Bombs of All Time. All right, let's check out this bunch of losers ...

10. Star Wars. Silly little tale of battling spaceships and fuzzy, one-dimensional characters shooting ray guns. Lucas was so desperate for wooden characters he cast two robots in leading roles. Over the top FX detract from any semblance of story. Harrison Ford is ridiculous as a space cowboy; gimme a break. Princess Leia *(Carrie Fisher)* wears a laughable black bun on her head and packs a pistol. Series continued strictly for kiddies in five increasingly bizarre sequels.

(Rollie grasps his head and wails in despair, falling down on the table again).

9. Lord of the Rings. Tiresome re-telling of Tolkien's meandering mishmash of an imaginary universe and clumsy metaphor for the meaning of life, all centered around a perversely hypnotic and symbolic piece of jewelry. Producers stripped together footage to spread out

three movies in order to recoup their ill-fated investment. Don't miss the silly Mr. Natural-like wizard, riding a stallion and holding a big stick. Moses or Rooster Cogburn, charging on a galloping stead.

8. Gone With The Wind. Weeper about the old South, at once an apologia for slaveholders, a fantasy about a neverland of goofy romantics, and an overwrought big screen epic that fizzled with the critics. Vivien Leigh's selfish and spoiled protagonist gets no sympathy; nor does Clark Gable's unprincipled opportunist. A downer of an ending closes an overlong bust that nevertheless drew a depression-era escapist audience and still endures as a piece of camp nostalgia and evidence of the foregone moonlight and magnolias movie mogul style.

7. Jaws. Silly scare flick about an overly big shark made of rubber and three Quixote-like protagonists. Inexplicably, young director Steven Spielburg substitutes real fright scenes for the nothingness of open water and an old-fashioned eerie soundtrack that sounds like a plugged-in flugelhorn. Where's the beef, Steven? Or should we say, where's the rubber? Once the audience finally, at last, sees the creature, they are immediately barraged with gore and violence. Yuk!

6. The Exorcist. Bizarre yarn about a devil-possessed kid who nauseates the audience by spinning her head and spouting pea soup. Oscar nomination for Ellen Burstyn for keeping a straight face while looking worried.

5. Pulp Fiction. Quentin Tarrantino's time-confused mess seeks to emulate the quaint set-ups of Reservoir Dog with disastrous effects. Revolting sequences of bestiality and violence underscore a dismally failed effort that will be a humorous object lesson in film schools for a long time.

4. Raging Bull. Robert DeNiro's disgusting character shocked enough for an Oscar win even as the pathological melancholia and brutish interludes prove too much for critics and audiences alike. Part of Scorcese's morose period.

3. The Wizard of Oz. Dreamy-eyed farm girl fantasizes and learns an obvious life lesson when her imagination runs wild during a tornado and she is time-transported to a gaily-decorated soundstage full of midgets and flying monkeys. Strictly kid fare.

2. It's A Wonderful Life. Fanciful tale of a depressed man who gets better after a chance encounter with a street tramp who claims to be an angel. A mauldin, sentiment-drenched ending states the obvious in an abysmal effort at high drama. A camp classic.

And number one, the biggest bomb of all time ... Citizen Kane. Orson Welles and his radio-idiots ran amok with RKO money in this unintentional laugher that guaranteed no one would ever take the studio seriously again. Weird and disconcerting camera angles and close-ups keep the audience fidgety in this nearly unwatchable curiosity that proved to Hollywood moguls that rampant creativity could scuttle the best of studio projects, in this case the effort to expose the Hearst empire, the movie industry's longtime protagonist which controlled the world's celluloid supply. Depression from this epic failure forever blunted Welles' career and he ate too much and gained a lot of weight.

(Rollie lifts his head from the table, an amazed expression, and suddenly laughs uproariously.)

Well ...that's it, folks. I'm laughing so hard the tears are running down my leg. Hey! And it's really rough on the hosiery. Time's up. This is Midge Dewey, sitting in for Rollie Allgood and ... well, it may not actually ever happen again. Now for a news break. *(flips switch, sits stunned and looking at the paper.)* I never knew this guy was so funny. Isn't he? I was supposed to play this for laughs ... Maybe it's better I didn't ... Or ... Did I?

Chip: *(rushing into the room)* That's the funniest thing I've ever heard. But where the hell did it come from? *(Sergio walks into the room unnoticed, wide-eyed).*

Midge: Well, here it is. I just read the damned thing. It's a hoot, huh? I coulda set it up better if I had realized it was a farce.

Chip: *(taking the papers)* Well ... this don't look like Rollie's work to me. *(He turns and looks at Sergio, standing there with a big smile.)*

Sergio: Thank you. Thank you. I am a writer. Will I get paid more? Chip: You ...Wrote this?

Sergio: Ah yes, and also this one. I have just finished. *(holds up papers)* Chip: You ... wrote another one?

Sergio: Well, boom and bust and boobs, bombs and bombshells. I got very confused. And so I wrote them ... two ways *(holds up two fingers)* That way, I think, there is no way to lose. But ... I was so surprised that you just ... put it on. Writing must be ... easy ... if you don't need the sleep.

(A voice comes through the wall speaker)

Sybil: Chip, this is Sybil at the front desk. We are getting a lot of calls ... and I've got Mr. Allgood for you on line 5. He ... sounds agitated but ... he's laughing too.

Chip: *(pushing speaker button)* Sybil?

Sybil: Yes.

Chip: These are confusing times. Put him on and we'll see what we can make of it.

(Scene goes to dark.)

SCENE THREE: *(Scene opens in Sergio's old office, with a teenaged punk-decorated young intern poring over press packets on the desk. Three characters come walking through, on their way to lunch, pulling on their coats, Rollie, Chip, and finally Sergio appears.)*

Rollie: I've been wanting us to move into comedy for some time. Now with Sergio on board we can launch a comedy showcase, with videos, audios ...

Chip: You like your new office, Sergio? Hey, a window and everything. If your new show doesn't work out, you can take a flying leap ... into the shrubbery way below.

Sergio: I have to go by the post office and send some money home.

(As they walk out, Sergio turns to look at the punk kid by his former desk. He is standing there looking at him almost defiantly.)

Dietrich: Hey, dude. You can call me Dietrich. Do us both a favor and feast on this. *(thrusts papers at Sergio)*

Sergio: Well ... I'd like to help you out.

Dietrich: Thanks, man. It's just a coupla drawings for some characters and a little description. And ... I got 'em up here too *(taps his head)* I am a writer, man, a writer! This is just a temp gig down here.

Sergio: *(looking intently at the caricatures.)* Beevis ... and ... Butthead... Junior?

Dietrich: Right.

Sergio: ... meet ... Juno?

Dietrich: Imagine that, dude?

Sergio: *(tucks them in his pocket)* I ... will see what I can do.

Dietrich: Think of that trio, dude. A ménage au trow, know what I mean? It could be adult only, you know, or it could be PG-13 anyway. Juno gets preggers and ... whose is it? Huh? Yeah, man! It's like a mystery farce.

Sergio: Yes, that would be a new genre.

Dietrich: And that's good, ain't it? *(Noise from outside)*

Chip: Hey! I'm famished here.

Sergio: Coming! I used to work here by the way. I ... will read it."

Dietrich: It's a hit, dude. You'll see it. *(points at pages)* Yeah, I mean … yeah … you'll see it. It's all in the ink … on the page.

Sergio: *(making his way out)* You know … We all see things in a different way, Mr. Dietrich, so nothing is what it seems, not really. It's only what it seems to us. *(exits)*

Dietrich: *(stands alone for few seconds and then saunters back to his modest desk. He sits glumly silent for a moment, thoughtful, then jumps alert.)* She's not preggers. No! She's smuggling ten kilos of Pineapple Express. Yeaaaaaaaaah! *(he grabs his pad and writes furiously.)*

by Jim Cleveland

OUTER PATHS

There is a litmus for luminosity
linked to the defeat of animosity
something to do with possibly
stepping away from pomposity

There is a luminous path that logically
cuts from the road of bellicosity
something to do with the velocity
in which we speed from hypocrisy

There is an oracle emoting obliquely
moving opelisks of aura completeness
our opulent, moving treatise
of life's potential sweetness.

There are all things integrally related
a reality overcoming the sedated
whose minds show nothing not indicated
within the material derivative, and placated

Futures break through these incisions
collapsing bars piled there in derision
of former gangs of grunts in this prison
surging to some spiritual collision

YOUR WILL FOR FREE

Free Will. It determines the fate of nations.
Free Will. It's the key to all relations.
Free Will. Makes us do it right and wrong.
Free Will. Every day we sing its song.

Free Will. It's a blessing, could be much worse.
Free Will. From the rocking cradle to the rolling hearse.
Free Will. God gives it; men take it away.
Free Will. Protect it or let your mind decay.

Free Will. It pilots your life's great journey.
Free Will. It drives all the learning.
Free Will. It poses many action questions.
Free Will. It chooses all your directions.
And informs your every affection.

Inside your heart,
Inside your mind,
Inside your body deep,
There is a force
That runs the course
Within your life's full sweep.
It's yours for free,
Can be lost by degree,
So hold it precious close.
Defend it well,
Make it not for sale.
That's a vital key.

Manifestations and Mollifications

SCENE ONE: *The offices of Imperial Publishing Co., St. Louis, MO., in 1894. Two well-dressed men walk into room.*

J.T. Marcum: I don't care what your newspaper says. I have the technological miracle of the century ... right here in this office.

Richard Swiney: The railroad? Does the intercontinental rail run through here, then? *(Smirks, draws imaginary line in the air as he walks by.)*

Marcum: Sir, you know that the railroad can only take you to the west coast. I can bring it back. I can hold the entire spectrum of this vast and glorious country in my hands. *(Gripping the air with a fist.)*

Swiney: Ah! Then, you have a telephone, of course. Indeed, what could be more wondrous than talking to someone in another city through a ... wire? Does anyone really understand how that works?

Marcum: That, Richard, is only a transported voice, as marvelous as it is. Imperial Publishing offers even more. You could call it a ... multi-medium.

(He has knelt in front of a safe and is turning the dial. He opens the door and pulls forth a large black portfolio case, which he places on the desk.)

Swiney: Aha! What have we here in the ominous black case? Is it more powerful than a locomotive then? Faster than a racing telephone wire ... or a speeding bullet?

Marcum: You should be in Vaudeville, Richard. Or in a comic strip.

Swiney: I've been thinking about a cartoon character. I think the journalism money may be in the comics. Everybody likes to read the comics and if I can get the right character ... okay, so what's in the case?

Marcum: The number one technological miracle of this marvelous century is ... Photography.

(Opens the case and pulls forth several individually wrapped photographs in brown paper and places them carefully on his desk, then takes a large sheet of paper upon which words are printed.)

Swiney: I've seen photographs. I think Matt Brady shot every corpse in the war.

Marcum: Photography is much more than that. We have collected here quality images representing the length and breadth of this country. Look ... here ... this is called the Grand Canyon. Have you ever seen anything like that? You may not be able to go there, but with these large photographs we capture all of the grandeur, all of the magnificence. And here ... here is a trading post in the Indian Territory. And this one ... a scene of Negroes posed beside their cabin somewhere in northern Alabama. Look at this. These are the odd dwellings one sees in the cliffs out in the southwest. We have hundreds of photographs!

Swiney: It must be a breathtaking collection.

Marcum: Just a sample. We are about to astound the publishing world. Let me just read from our first page. This tells it eloquently. *(Begins to read from the frontispiece.)* Our Own Country. That is the name. It tells our dear readers that this is their country, they own a piece of it, right here on these pages, and in times to come, it will be their manifest destiny to travel and see it all. In the meantime, well, here, let me read: Our Own Country, representing our native land and its Splendid Natural Scenery. Rivers, Lakes, Waterfalls, Geysers, Glaciers, Mountains, Canyons, and ... Entrancing Landscapes reproduced in Royal Purple Colors with Graphic Historical Descriptions and Character Sketches ... constituting a complete historic and geographic Picturesque America ... By James Cox ... Author of ... and a list of his other books, including Missouri at the World's Fair. I believe you reviewed that one for us, and thank you!

Swiney: Well, it's all more dramatic than the telephone, I suppose.

Marcum: It's like you are there. Look at the crisp, sharp detail of these images. And Richard, the point is that the steam engine locomotive is just a means to an end. The telephone provides only utility. But photography combines the power of the image with the power of the book, the written word, and emulates the art of the finest galleries ... and one can hold all this in the hands. It is of beauty and substance. Like the Scriptures in a way. They make religion a reality. We, here, can make a reality out of this entire magnificent country and ... well, that's a valuable product, now, isn't it?

Swiney: But there is the question, sir. At what price can you sell this book? What is the market? The rich only? It will cost a king's ransom to produce it ... won't it?

Marcum: We have investors ... partners, actually ... in New York.

Swiney: Yankees then.

Marcum: *(after a pause)* Well, yes. They won the war; they have the money. We must work together now, to build this country.

Swiney: Nonetheless ...

Marcum: Yes. Speak freely.

Swiney: They may have the money, but you'd better watch your own pocketbook if you are intent upon dealing with those people.

Marcum: I shall tread lightly; believe me. There is a deep void of honor and integrity in the North, no greater evidence than the way brutes like Sherman and Grant laid waste to the Southland. Nevertheless ... If one wants money, one must go to the banks.

Swiney: Well, your photographs are incredible. They are certain to see the potential.

Marcum: And you, Richard, can be a part of this. The main reason I show you these is that I want to hire you myself. I would offer you a position in marketing and beyond that, to build good will with the people, north, south, east and west. It will be like a new profession in a way, working for Imperial, raising our profile and our image of greatness. It will be like an educational promotion business that we might call something like ... Public Relationships.

Swiney: Like ... sociology.

Marcum: Well ... like sociology developed into salesmanship.

Swiney: Assisting people in ... thinking correctly.

Marcum: Yes ... so to speak. And then buying accordingly.

Swiney: Like combining the advertising department with the editorial department then?

Marcum: Good grief, Richard. Must you always think like a journalist. Your paper is no less capitalist than we are, and we will pay you better.

Swiney: Well, when would we make it happen?

Marcum: Anytime ... soon ... of course, after your favorable review of "Our Own Country" comes out.

Swiney: And ... I'm sure you'll want to be in the Sunday edition ... with our big comics section. Marcum: And so what's your big funny paper idea then?

Swiney: Well he's like a big muscle guy, from another planet. He's got a colorful suit and wears a cape. He can fly, maybe. He comes down and fights for all the stuff we love. Maybe call him Super Dupper Man.

Marcus: Name's too long.

Swiney: Yeah?

Marcus: Yeah.

Swiney: Maybe I'll just call him ... Dupper!   *(Scene goes to dark)*

SCENE TWO: *The same office. A new desk has appeared at left. A nameplate reads "Richard A. Swiney, Pubic Relations." He walks in, with an overall-clad workman trudging behind him. He picks up the nameplate and thrusts it at him.*

Swiney: It's public relations. Public relations. We're not running a brothel, here, Oscar. You will have to get it re-made.

Oscar: Kinda funny though, ain't it? Pubic Relations. Ha! I think of them little kinky black hairs.

Swiney: Thank you, Oscar.

Oscar: It ain't funny?

Swiney: Well, it does describe my preferred nighttime activities, though hopes are not always brought to fruition.

(Oscar leaves. Swiney has barely sat down before Marcum storms through the doorway, with a secretary in tow.)

Marcum: Well, they've pulled the financing, Richard. The money is gone. We're in the toilet with presses poised to run.

Swiney: Whatever for? The collection is unprecedented.

Marcum: It's not the photography. Oh, no. They loved the photography. They asked me if I got Stonewall Jackson to write the copy. I was stunned. I said, he's dead. No, they said, he must be part of the Confederacy underground, right here in our offices.

Swiney: Mr. Cox? He wrote a compelling narrative.

Marcum: They said they are offended ... to the core, they say. Look at this. *(tosses a crumpled fold of paper onto Swiney's desk)* Their hearts are bleeding, they say, because of our insensitivity. They say we defame the Negroes, that we insult the God-forsaken Indians. Imagine. Those savages have been warring us for years, killing innocent homesteaders. Illiterate, unsanitary, unprincipled savages. And we've defamed them!

Swiney: *(poring through the pages)* Well, they've set forth some specific passages here. Maybe we could just get some revisions made and go forward. Mr. Cox will surely go along with it if it's going to sink the ship.

Marcum: I don't know that I can ask James to honor these wishes. They strike at the very core of our differences with the bloodsucking Yankees. They want to control everything, all of the wealth of this grand country. We fought a war over it, and we lost, and now they are worse than ever, even more in control of our destiny. The South continues to suffer; they continue to get richer. And now ... this ... telling us that we have to completely re-write our project to pay homage to their naïve little ... concerns and these ... idiotic empathies.

Swiney: They think it's condescending to pose these Negro children eating watermelon.

Marcum: They love watermelon. It was just a great way to round them up and get them recorded. You ever try to get a bunch of kids to stay still for a photograph? Hell, they got free watermelon.

Swiney: We have two Negroes at the newspaper now. Well ... they are saying ... says here ... that we're promoting slavery. Are we doing that? How can they think such a thing?

Marcum: Because they cannot see clearly what is on the line without bias against the South. The Confederates killed so ... fuckin' many of them. Because they will not see the reality of life as it is, the races, the ... circumstances. They refuse to see our New South realities and the balanced society we are seeking to create in which each of the races builds it own character, its own destiny, among its own kind, in the spirit of competitive capitalism that ... these people in New York claim to represent.

Swiney: Slavery is gone, J.T. It's gone. We'll get nowhere saying anything good about it at all, or denigrating colored people ... or like always puttin' them in the back of the line. And that's what people are doing. I see it all over town.

Marcum: But the facts don't lie, Richard. *(Steps over and takes the pages from Swiney)* Listen to this. This is reality. This is what they could understand if they got their fat asses out of their New York ... jungle ... and came out into the country to see just what their war of aggression against the South has really done for the colored man. We deal honestly with this. And I quote from our book: "Readers of sensationalist literature naturally look upon the colored slave of the south as a kind of misery. A mention of him conjures up in their mind thoughts of whipping posts, impossible tasks, insufficient food and clothing, and treatment just one degree worse than that accorded to the horses and cattle of the plantation. This idea is almost entirely erroneous." Imperial will tell it like it is. Quote again. "Men are always to be found in every walk of life who will take advantage of opportunities and ignore their responsibilities, and there were, of course, many planters, traders and overseers who were guilty of occasional, and even systematic brutality." Certainly, we can be honest about this. Continuing ... "But the majority of the slaves were perfectly content, and their loyalty was surprising." This is absolutely true! The Yankees won't admit it. They've got to justify their rapacious plunder. Skip down ... skip down. Here is a photograph of an old Negro with an ax. "The old man whose portrait appears on this page works a great deal harder to keep body and soul together now than he ever did in his slavery days. He misses the care and protection which were always his under the old regime, and if his memories of servitude include an occasional act of severity, he does not enlarge upon these details of his past history." Bygones should be bygones, Richard, north and south. Quoting again ..."Chopping wood is his sole source of income, and were it not for the fact that his wants are few, they would very infrequently go unfilled." Now, this is the kind of truth the Yankees just don't want to hear about.

Swiney: J.T., the war is over. You didn't win. You just need to do what you need to do to get the money and get the book out. It's the money, you know. That's what it's all about.

Marcum: Whose side are you on? The Yankee capitalists, I reckon.

Swiney: The side with the money. It always wins. Just ... write something else. Have him write something else.

Marcum: *(pauses, with frown)* Do you really think the war is over? ... because it's not. Swiney: Get the money then, J.T. Then you'll have something to fight with.

Marcum: *(after a long pause, turns to the secretary who has been waiting patiently with pad and pencil, now speaking more calmly, thoughtfully)* Mrs. Carmichael, I need to send a telegram to New York, and I want to get a courier over to Mr. Cox's house with an invitation to dinner.

Mrs. Carmichael: To your home, sir?

Marcum: No, the Beef House, the finest joint in the city. You'll join us, Richard. I may need your powers of ... public persuasion. That's what we should call your new profession, Richard. Public Persuasion.

Swiney: No.

Marcum: No?

Swiney: That would tip our hand.

Marcum: *(disdainfully)* Is that ... journalist thought?

Swiney: Well, didn't Cox write this for the money in the first place? I don't think unreconstructed Confederates are any more disdainful of money than you are, J.T.

Marcum: He'll fuss and fume. But we'll have plenty of bourbon on hand. Mrs. Carmichael, by the way, send a fifth of scotch along with the dinner invitation. He likes scotch.

Swiney: Now, you're talking. Now that's public relations. Maybe it'll be pubic relations too. Ha!

Marcum: *(sighs)* And it's part of the compromises we will no doubt find in the book publishing business as we go forward, Richard, and in all the myriad of future applications for photographic imagery that are to come. The New Yorkers think they will control book publishing in America, and the new technologies, but it'll be a cold day in hell before we in St. Louis allow that to happen.

Swiney: Mr. Marcum ... I think I'm going to call him Captain Super.

Marcum: What? He's in the military? Are we getting invaded then?

Swiney: Well, no. I just thought it gave him ... authority.

Marcum: Captain Super. That's redundant as hell. What is it you're trying to create here, a super man?

Swiney: Well, yeah. Something like that. I know the right name will pop out if I just keep thinking about it.

Marcum: I guess a super man needs a super name. Gotta have one, really. Got to have a focus on something simple.

Swiney: Yeah, and sometimes the obvious can be right under your nose and you can't see it.

(The two characters look at each other thoughtfully. The stage goes dark)

GOD ALA CARTE

You can sing high hosannas
Lift your praise into the sky.
You can dream of gold in heaven
If by some rules you will abide.

You can bask in high cathedrals
With colored glass and ringing bells
You can heed those admonitions
To keep it pure and avoid hell

You can send your preachers to Africa
Give your baskets to the poor
You can save the soup can wrappers
And find your church a bright allure

You can pray for all the sinners
Stay away from foolish highs
You can draw the line of good and bad
Say that spirit will one day rise.

But if you never know a personal God
The seed of Love inside your heart
If you never talk to your Creator
If you daily live apart
Then you're missing all the feeling
For life is more than the breathing.
It's the daily choice of love Ala Carte
God is always there to talk to, Ala Carte

by Jim Cleveland

HIGHER MOMENTS

Look around you, be the moment
For that's all there really is.
Tomorrow's just a notion, yesterday just a potion
That makes us what we are by what we did.
Look around you; see your loved ones
Appreciate them as they are
Tomorrow they'll be gone; yesterday's already gone
And this moment is all that lives and gives us fire.
There is spirit in the moment we're looking higher.

You can't go back to some yesterday
Here, around you, is what it is.
Things could have been, maybe should have been
But what you have here is what really is.

You can't just dream of tomorrow's wins
Here, around you, is what is actual.
To get to anywhere you have to know
That each moment is a fractional.

You should not bury in another time
In places of thoughtless ritual
Be yourself, each second in its place
And rejoice in your spiritual nuptials

I've known some people who yearned to be
What they used to be or could be
Yet what they are and how they are
Is right in front of me.
What you're looking for, my brother,
Is what's looking here at you.
What you're looking for
Is looking back at you
In the moment you can see it
Through and through

ESCAPING IRAQ
(and other depressed areas)

CAST OF CHARACTERS

J.B. Hypestein, CEO of a Hollywood movie studio.
Puffy Seams, An agent and promoter.
Kurt Russell, lookalike
Goldie Hawn, lookalike
Secretary

SCENE ONE: *The office of movie mogul J.B. Hypestein. He sits mulling over papers, puffing on a cigar. A secretary opens the door to usher in an anxious and wide-eyed fat man in a rumpled suit.*

Secretary: Mr. Seams. *(She speaks coldly and closes the door quickly.)*

JB: Five minutes, Puffy. Going on four.

Puffy: Escape from Iraq! *(He flourishes his fat arms widely, emulating a marquee.)*

JB: I told you, it's too early to make money on that. The industry is just now getting to 9.11. Whatever it is, forget it.

Puffy: But … ain't the war winding down? The Democrats got in.

JB: Puffy, it ain't over 'til it's over. We've got investments in the infrastructure over there, Halliburton and the boys. They've got to have protection. We can't expect the mercenaries to carry the whole load.

Puffy: C'mon J.B. Let's just carry some of it over here. Surely, the Bush folks don't mind if we do a little action flick about their war.

JB: Well, they just don't wanna be in it, that's the problem. Who the hell does want to be in it and what's it about? Sum it up quick.

Puffy: Think … Big Beauty and Big Lips! JB: I give up. Mick and Bianca Jagger?

Puffy: Angelina Jolie! Look, JB, she's interested. Picture it. She's a nurse, a busty one, kind of a super nurse, with a big gun somewhere. She loves the Iraqi kiddos, rustles up a bunch of imperiled ones for a mad dash to the Syrian border, with wild-eyed ragheads in hot pursuit. It's like a Blood Diamond, Apocalypto, Babel, and Tomb Raider kind of piece. And the ultimate timely angle. We can get a lot of free publicity out of all that adoption stuff she's been doing, you know, with the orphans and refugees and stuff.

JB: We don't usually like to have kids on the set either, but there could be some photo ops. Keep talking.

Puffy: That's not all, J.B. Here's another thought for you ... Snake!

JB: Ummm. Giant serpents living under the dunes, maybe even mutated into monsters by the toxicity of the ... who knows, radioactive bomb waste or something.

Puffy: No! Snake Pleskin, back in black, eyepatch and all, star of Escape from New York and Escape from LA and also very much interested in such a project.

JB: I thought Goldie had him lined up for some comedy crap, over at Disney.

Puffy: He's interested all right. One more pix and we can do Escape in a boxed set. And we're still revising the Escape from Sedona script, remember?

JB: Sedona baloney. Giant Red Rocks coming alive and attacking a colony of teenage mystics? Better stay with the Iraq idea. But ... I'm having a little trouble with the Russell-Jolie mix.

Puffy: Well, he's a mercenary, of course, but turns out to be a hero, you know, like Bogie in Casablanca, and he comes in to save the ragtag caravan and all the kids, but with Jolie herself killing off a lot of bad guys too. I'd say they need to kill off about the same number. Gender equality. She's got to protect her super girl image but Snake is not the kind of character who would take kindly to a woman killing off more cretins than him.

JB: The dead counts can be worked out. What about the contracts? I need some assurance they're both interested and I don't see either damned one of their agents in the room. Just what is it you're offering here?

Puffy: Well, Kurt's agent said if I could get Angelina, he'd likely do it. Goldie's agent said it might be okay if she can hang around and chaperone and the money's right. Angelina's agent says she'll do it if she gets lots of kissing and killing and plenty of close-ups with amber desert light.

JB: Ummmm. Sounds like some potential for hedonistic disaster here. Maybe we could get Goldie busy on another movie, in another location. Remember that red carpet orgy with Billy Bob?

Puffy: How about the Gidget remake? Gidget goes to Tijuana. That hasn't started shooting.

JB: My God, Puffy, Goldie's a grandmother. She can't do Gidget, besides there are several nude scenes, with the gila monster. We've got a hot new chick for Gidget. I discovered her right here on this large black sofa just like week. Haw!

Puffy: Well, Vince was thinking you were going to write in an older woman monster-in-law part, maybe. Like the voice of comedic conscience when they get to boy's town.

JB: Well, we had Judi Dench in mind for that one to get that kind of Bitch and Queen in the brothel dichotomy idea into the movie, you know. But maybe Goldie would do a whore. She hasn't won an Oscar yet, after all. A kind of blonde ditzy wisecracking whore could be worked in, especially if we can get her off the Escape from Iraq set.

Puffy: Yeah, hey, she could have this thing, you know, like when these Mexican boys start to climb on, she purrs seductively, but dramatically: Sock it to me. Umm. Sock it to me.

JB: She won't do that, you moron. This is a drama. And … Come to think of it, since it's just an escape picture, we don't have to get involved in politics. We're just getting the hell out of the country. It's like a morality tale.

Puffy: I suppose it's also like, you know, a metaphor. Maybe the critics will like it. They appreciate it when one thing really means something else. That way they can say the usual thing, the world is confused, and it's because we make it confusing, and aren't we smart to figure that one out.

JB: Idiot. Maybe the love scenes mean that in Iraq somebody is getting screwed, huh?

Puffy: Yeah, like everybody, but hey, speaking of that, then we can fuel the Jolie and Russell romance gossip, and then the tabloids will suck in Goldie and we'll be off to the bank again.

JB: Maybe so. Maybe there is really is some money to be made off Iraq … even without having to go over there, which can be fatal to your health.

Puffy: Yeah, and to give it a little Babel, Iowa Jima Letters, Apocalypto class, we'll throw in some other languages with subtitles. That's getting' kinda trendy.

JB: We'll have to wait and see how to pitch it, whether it's to an audience that reads, or wants to. There's an axiom that you can't mix action and captions. Somebody could be reading a subtitle and could miss a decapitation or something. And you know how expensive it can be to stage one of them. And the last time we did one, Wynona Ryder fainted right there on the set.

Puffy: I think the guys up at Speciality Arts in Culver City do the best job with that effect. Whaddya you think?

JB: They're okay, but they sure screwed up some of the splattering bullets in Dumb Action Movie III. And this is really going to be an important bullet picture. It's in Iraq, for God's sake.

(The intercom rings. The secretary's voice comes through)

Secretary: Mr. Hypestein, Mr. Russell and Miss Hawn here to see you. They were just in the ... neighborhood and were hoping for a few moments.

(JB stares at Puffy, who stares back.)

Puffy: *(softly)* Holy Shit!

JB: What's this about?

(Puffy shrugs theatrically.)

JB: Certainly, send them in.

(Kurt Russell and Goldie Hawn look-alikes are ushered into the office with smiles and handshakes all around.)

JB: Well, sit down. Sit down. I can't believe you're here. We were just talking about a new movie project ... actually a couple of new movie projects and your names quickly came to mind.

Goldie: *(theatrically, staring right in his face to get his attention)* Escape from Afghanistan!

JB: I beg your pardon.

Kurt: Goldie as a courageous aid worker saving street children in Afghanistan. Billy Bob Thornton is interested in playing an anti-hero type. It's like an orphanage fortress and they fight off the Taliban.

JB: Goldie ... with an automatic weapon?

Kurt: Playing against type, sure! Even an RPG.

JB: The word "bomb" comes to mind. I just think ...

Kurt: I know what you're going to say. I should be in it too, but I can't.

JB: You can't?

Kurt: I've got this truly amazing script for you. It's a family picture about courageous nurses adopting imperiled orphans in Iraq. I can co-star.

Puffy: And ... who else?

Kurt: It's a maybe, but a strong maybe. Picture this, guys. Are you ready? Puffy: I can't be sure.

(Goldie giggles. Kurt plays up the moment.)

JB: Yes?

Kurt: Big Lips!

(The room falls to silence. Then J.B. speaks softly, confidently.)

JB: We're way ahead of you, big man. Puffy has talked to Angelina and I think she's in. It's gonna be a great match-up.

Kurt: Angelina?

Puffy: Uh ... JB ... I don't know if I really ...

Goldie: Oh, no! Hell, no. Kurt isn't working with that ... woman! Oh, no! We've talked about that.

Kurt: Sorry ... sorry ... no, I meant the Mick.

Puffy: Mick?

Goldie. Right! Exactly!

Kurt: Mick Jagger. He's about ready to do another picture and the treatment appealed to him. The Stones aren't touring.

JB: Did you mean ... Mick Jagger? I thought you said courageous nurses.

Kurt: That's the cool thing. We're cross dressers. Me and Mick. That's how we sneak into the hospital. It's a buddy picture! But with a big twist. Kind of Transamerica in Iraq. And we're trying to get that Abigail kid, you know, from Little Miss Sunshine. On the road to Turkey, all kinds of kooky, crazy things happen, like kind of a lighter-hearted Blood Diamond, you know, and there's a crosseyed camel that smells really bad and has gas.

Puffy: It's a comedy? An Iraq comedy? JB: Smells like Ishtar.

Kurt: Goldie thinks it'll be a hoot. And .. and .. and we can line up a pink Hummer for the escape vehicle. Wow! And we're gonna work in a little animal of some kind, can't have kids without a pet, huh?

JB: Sounds like a parody of Ishtar.

Goldie: Well, I don't know why you're so negative. It's pretty obvious to me that things are downright bleak over there. Yukaroonie! It all needs to be ... lightened up! That whole ... geographical area needs to be lightened up. It's much too depressing over there. Just ... depressing. *(Everyone stares at Goldie, speechless)* Well. anyway ... I think that should be obvious to anybody.

Puffy: *(after a pause)* Did they? ... Did they say for sure that they could ... make a pink Hummer?

(JB puffs his cigar vigorously and smoke fills the room. Characters stare at one another as the stage goes dark.)

The Grit Corny-Act ... knows y'all, sees y'all.

The Answer is: Finding Neverland
The Question: What's the name of the biography written by Divine's masseuse?

Answer: The Fast and the Furious
The Question: Describe the survivors of a trip to the Baghdad airport.

Answer: Gone in 60 Seconds
Question: Describe the hopes and dreams of intellectuals when George W. Bush begins to speak.

Answer: Cold Mountain
Question: What was the bedroom atmosphere in the White House when Hillary learned about Monica?

Answer: The Incredibles, Shark Tales and Shrek
Question: Characterize Bush's WMD assertions in three different ways.

Answer: Abercrombies and Zombies
Question: Name two classes of people, one well-dressed and one not.

Answer: ET's, EKGs and English Peas
Question: Name two heart-rending experiences and a common garden vegetable.

Answer: What the Bleep Do We Know!?
Question: Describe the consensus view after a Bush cabinet meeting.

Answer: Apocalpyse Now
Question: Describe the impact of Fox News on legitimate journalism.

Answer: " .... the horror ... the horror ...."
Question: What is the O'Reilly Factor?

Answer: The Sound of Silence
Question: Describe our anticipations for Richard Wang's singing career.

Answer: Long Day's Journey into Night
Question: What is the title of the latest Iraq war assessment report?

Answer: Gone With The Wind
Question: What could happen if you stand behind an elephant with flatulence?

Answer: Shock and Awe
Question: Describe the feelings of most Americans on the price of war and the use of expensive weaponry to destroy things we must rebuild.

Answer: Babel
Question: Characterize the content of a Bush press conference.

Answer: Apocalypto
Question: What happens when terrorists bomb a disco?

Answer: Deadwood
Question: Describe the new career of Donald Rumsfeld.

Answer: The Wild Bunch
Question: Describe a bouquet gathered at a nature preserve.

Answer: Close Encounters of the Third Kind
Question: Describe Jennifer Lopez' latest marriage.

Answer: Pirates of the Caribbean
Question: Characterize the banking community in the Bahamas.

Answer: The Pope, Lassie and a seafood platter
Question: Name a priest, a beast and a feast.

Answer: Sherlock Holmes, John B. and Minestrone
Question: Name a snoop, a sloop and a soup.

Little Richard, Philosophical Giant
(It wouldn't have worked as Little Dick)

ANNOUNCER: Good evening. We're live here in Lagos, Nigeria, at the 69th annual conference of the International Association of Representational Simplism Philosophical Studies. Some of the world's leading simplistic philosophers are here tonight to pay tribute to perhaps the greatest of all time, the amazing Richard Penniman.

Stepping to the podium now, in a hushed hall, is our opening keynote speaker, the esteemed Professor Billy Boob Bradford of the Tennessee Institute of Philosophical Technology and Technical Physiology.

When the applause died, Professor Bradford was silent for a few seconds before addressing the assembled academicians, representing the finest universities on the planet. The scholar spoke deliberately, dramatically, with a twanging Southern accent:

A man called ... Little. An ironic, self-imposed title that followed him across a lifetime. An amazing persona, he at once presented himself in loud make-up and called himself, a dichotomy never understood by the minds of his day, but revealed in its brilliant simplicity by modern-day simplistic scholars.

The man's greatest contributions to our treasury of poetic philosophy are by no means little. They will endure the annals of time. They still shine brightly today in his blatantly, purposively simple, yet provocative and highly symbolic lyric statements that cut to the heart of all issues of his day and ours, leaving them bare, clear and naked as a peeled pear and exposing the inner core of true meaning that had to be disguised because of the terrifying social paradigms of his time, but can now bloom in pure simplistic flower in this modem age.

The power of his philosophy, his urgent message, was always shrouded, cloaked because of the peculiar social mores of his day, when everything in society was based upon getting paid and getting laid. While Richard adhered to the style, the powerful social and psychological exposes behind his simplicity ultimately have been discovered by scholars, hailed for their understated eloquence and universal pertinence, and even as the remedies for mankind to survive in the frenzied times that he displayed all too well in his frenzied explosions of pseudo piano playing that permeated all of his work.

But may I say, there were never any convoluted academic sentences such as mine for man they called Little Richard. He could cut to the core of all and make it sound as simple as a horny man and a world of dark holes in which to explore.

And so, in the several days ahead, you will hear scholars across the globe come together in glorious recognition of Little Richard, the amazing Richard Penniman, as the foremost social philosophy writer of his day, and founder of the philosophic school of simplistic scholarship in the days ahead, We will discuss his greatest works, including:

Tutti Fruitti: A global panel will discuss Richard's powerful anthem to ethnic peace, all races living in harmony, and analyze the ecstatic above and beyond language emotionalism of the immortal line from the song's amazing sidebar, "Wop Bop A Lou Wop A Lop Bam Boom!

This, dear colleagues, encapsulates and accurately predicts decades of violent Italian mob corruption in the U.S., years of murder and strife that faced us in the time of Richard s time. Wop Bop A Lou Wop A Lop Bam Boom. Violence ... racial slurring ... Be-Bop ... a kind of ethnic ice cream. This is a true masterpiece that says it all.

Slipping and Sliding: As the promises of civil rights failed to come to fruition, however, and died on the vine, the flip side of this philosophical treatise reveals a world of black people falling and failing in society again. "I'm gonna be your fool no more," wails Richard, and we understand, for we have been "peeping and hiding" too, not standing up to the moral code that we would ascribe to ourselves.

Good Golly, Miss Molly: When Richard first heard the horror of Molotov Cocktails, he was outraged. As he often does, Richard disguises the true theme into a love and lust story, as his record producers always insisted upon, but one can easily see that "sho likes to ball" indicates a ball of fire induced by the infamous "cocktail" and "can't hear yo' Mama call" plainly invokes the call of Mother Russia to disdain such insanity. We will remember that the Cold War with the Soviets was raging in those years.

Long Tall Sally: There has long been speculation of an affair with Sally Kellerman. But in another story, Sally is merely a euphemism for a shaft-like sex organ, which played a prominent role in Richard's life, and, in fact, in the lives of many of his contemporaries, and ours.

Jenny, Jenny: Who could forget "Jenny, Jenny, Jenny, spinnin' like a spinnin' top, Jenny, Jenny, Oh, Jenny Jenny," powerfully presenting the image of a spinning ballerina or ice skater. Never explained, these poignantly simple lyrics likely refer to Richard's first day in elementary school, in which he fell off the spinning-jinny, hit his head, and thought he was Buckwheat for several hours. Scholar researchers discovered the pivotal incident just last year while investigating the telltale word, "Oh" right in the middle of the Jenny . narrative, as if painfully being expelled from a flying fun vessel and being conked on the head and enticing the simplistic expression ... of pain.

Lucille: "You don't do yo' Daddy's will." Who could forget this one? An ode to TV's Lucille Ball, whose work Richard adored. She went 'the other way,' he often thought, when applying his make-up.

As an aside, he once emulated a famous I Love Lucy scene at a party by furiously stuffing chocolate candies in his mouth and down his shirt, and singing and playing piano with his feet at the same time.

It was a funny act but impractical for the stage as it made Richard fat, and it proved extremely difficult to sing with cheeks puffed by chocolate. On the second night, he slipped on a bon-bon and fell over an amplifier, and the experiment was over.

Heebie Jeebies: A cry for sanity in a world when everyone has the fabled "heebie jeebies" about the cold war and the bomb, and the klan, all exasperated by a of mind- altering drugs.

The Girl Can't Help It: A powerful statement about the irresistible hormonal drives of young people and their effects upon people searching for love.

Rip It Up: Richard's stylistic take on ghetto violence and the passions involved, again disguised, this time as Saturday night camaraderie. For the first time, ripping it up and balling it up were juxtaposed in the same context, and it led to the popular "having a ball" and "getting ripped" social terms and co-existent theories, built around parallel intoxications that may yet prove to be significantly related.

Ready Teddy: A call to a generation of young people to get ready and start building a new age. "Ready, set, go man, go, I got a gal that I love so." Here, Richard powerfully summarizes mankind's need to find soul mate couplings and then start out with energy and readiness together, in a world of excitement and challenge. The eternal challenge remains. Get laid, and build civilization. Richard knew it. Through his works, we know it too.

I Hear You Knockin': By any measure, the decades of Richard's definitive work are times of unfulfilled dreams, doors that don't get opened, and the secrets behind them. "I hear you knockin' but you can't come in. Come back tomorrow night and try it again." Howwwwwwwwww!" A cry of despair from a great philosopher, revealing the repetitive, time and time again frustration of our natures, fearful of opening doors, bloodied knuckles from the ones upon which we ourselves have rapped in our ravaged and rakish times of seeking and finding openings ... such as the ones we seek sexually in one another, the ones we see as openings for a wisecrack, and even those which open for us even deeper knowledge as we glean from Richard's work this week during our conference.

In addition to our lectures and panels, on Saturday night our Soul Food buffet will be followed by a Dress-Up Queen Party in which you are all urged to trans-dress and transpose yourself into a land of wonder and mirror balls while we preen and dance theatrically to all of Richard's favorites with special guest star impersonators including Eddie Murphy, Chris Rock, Cyndi Lauper and Billy Bob Thornton.

On Sunday, the Penniman Power Choir will perform choral renditions of Richard favorites. Richard himself will arrive in a white helicopter and walk the red carpet to the chapel pulpit where he will respond to our adulation and deliver a sermon which has tentatively been titled: Pianos and Pulpits: Theology and Sexual Philosophy As Dichotomies of My Life and Times.

On Sunday afternoon, we will join Richard at an outdoor barbeque and a special showing of "Down and Out in Beverly Hills" with a personal appearance by Fang, Richard's costarring feist dog protagonist.in the comedic film classic.

So I welcome you all to this meeting, our largest-ever gathering, in a time when we are seeing the concept of Simplism, the philosophy of succinct symbolism, growing in esteem throughout the academic world.

In concluding my remarks, I simply quote from another of Mr. Penniman's prophetic works: "All around the world ... rock and roll is here to stay." And so are we, my friends and colleagues, until Monday anyway. Checkout time is 11 a.m.

(Crashing noise in audience).

Announcer: *Oh, my. As Professor Bradford was finishing his remarks, a professor in the third row seems to have dozed off and fallen from his seat. I believe he hit his head, hard, on the seat in front of me.*

Bradford: "Is that man, okay? "Is he okay? Do we need a doctor? How 'bout an am-bu-lance?" "Oh! Please. Hit me again," wailed the man, "I can still hear him!"

LOVE ABOVE THE LITTER

Well, I paused to think about
What would make this day go better.
Seems like my dreams
And also my schemes
Have gotten fettered
Tiring to look at
and all weather-beaten
And tattered.

And I began to think about
What word would describe
That richly rolling vibe
That can lift you from inside
When desire wells up
to fill your cup
With sweet wine.

Well, the nice folks call it making love
While the crude ones call it the F-word.
Biologists talk about copulation
Preachers rail about fornication
Sitcoms turn it into gossip overheard

Teenagers think it heavenly honey
Pornographers call it easy money
Psychologists think it's worth analysis
Monks and nuns have put it to paralysis
Stand-ups twist it all to make it funny.

So after I had paused to consider
All that superfluous false glitter
I realized that my deeper dreams
Should replace my mental schemes
With a fresh start
And dump the smarmy litter.

Loving humans are beautiful creations
Fostering the plan for future generations
Rising above crude contemplations
Embracing the peace of higher relations
Above the dogma, above the false sheen
Love within, without and in-between.

The Return of Forrest Grump

SCENE ONE: *The Hollywood offices of Golan-Gobus-Garbleus-Goofus Productions, a studio which makes bloody potboilers.*

"Forrest Gump has a twin brother -- and we've got him! How's that for a grabber, J.B.?" Agent Puffy Seams was agitated, his arms spread wide in gesture. His fatness filled much of the space in front of the big man's desk.

Enswathed in a shroud of cigar smoke, J.B. wasn't so sure. "How do we know this guy's authentic? There's a lot of weirdos out in the weeds who just wanna cash in."

Like us, Puffy thought. But he said instead: "We got the papers. It's him, all right. Little goody two-shoes mom just dispatched him to an orphanage because she couldn't handle two of 'em. When he found out about it, he was mortified having to claim kin with a mental defective so he just laid low. He thinks it shows genetic deficiency. Even changed his name to Grump."

"So who is this guy, Einstein or something?"

"Close. I.Q. way up there. Brilliant, but cold, calculating, p.o.'ed all the time, doesn't trust anybody. Thinks the world is going to hell in a handbasket. Thinks nobody's any good."

"So where's he been lately, hiding in a cave or something?"

"No, not at all," Puffy wheezed, wiping the sweat off his fat, bald head. He's with the IRS, heads up the Omaha Division.

"Yeah," J.B. squinted. "That explains it. So, at least we can get him in here to talk ..... maybe come up with a script. It's gotta be R rated, though, or we won't be loyal to our audience. Think we can make this guy out to be pure evil?"

"Um-m, yeah. That shouldn't be much of a stretch."

SCENE TWO: *Same office. Same characters, ushering in a taciturn, precisely dressed businessman, every hair in place, training gym fit, with the cold hard eyes of a serial bureaucrat.*

J.B. offers scotch from a crystal decanter, speaking as he settles back. "There's an awful lot of potential here, Mr. Grump. Your brother's film grossed so much there was a sucking sound heard all over middle America." He laughed uproariously and settled back. "This is the golden age of sequels. I'm sure we can come up with one."

The cold eyes struck him and Grump spoke: "You're like all the life-sucking leeches who live by greed and malice. All the while you're manifesting your nature of violent animal territorialism that has long been abetted and encouraged in you by the DNA changes that Satan and his crowd made in you."

Puffy coughed nervously. J.B. attempted to smile but lost the thread. "Well, you know. We all got to make a living. I mean this is a legitimate business here. What's wrong with making a few bucks together?"

"What you're manifesting, you are. That's why I've consciously made myself superior to you all. You are all inferior, and you all cheat on your taxes. I just don't have time to catch everybody."

"Well now, wait a minute, Mr. Grump. There's no need for animosity. I just wanna make a picture of your life. You can tell your story. We give you the celluloid, the professional assistance so to speak. What is it you wanna say? I mean, we've already said the world is full of ... you know what ... at this studio anyway. I mean, we've done our part. The world's crazy, full of evil, injustice. Let's tell 'em about it. You'll make a few bucks. We'll make a few bucks. We'll be doing a public service."

"Why should I want to do anything for people? Mankind is hopeless and you're the prime example of it. I mean, these pitiful efforts to find spiritual truth in my poor brother's ignorance. No more than a romantic fantasy fomented by people who can't live in the real world. Talk about exploitation!"

"Yeah .... right, said J.B. uncertainly. "Fantasy. What the people need is a dose of just how bad this place really is. Why, I heard after the Zemeckis piece, there were people actually wanting to be retarded. A guy in Arkansas even tried to get a lobotomy. Talk about your bad influences."

Grump's eyes were steely, sharp. "I will do it," he said, "but I want to direct."

Puffy laughed nervously and wiped again. J.B. chuckled and spoke more compromisingly gentle.

"And I'm sure you'd be a fine director, but, see, we got these people on the payroll. They're directors and you know I gotta pay 'em anyway, so let's leave the directing to directors. You can be the Associate Producer. And, of course, you need to help us come up with a story of some kind. Need to have some conflict, you know, resolution, a couple or three climaxes here and there, lots of destruction of stuff, one of our well-endowed women actresses, of course, got to have a love interest. Say, have you met any of the ladies here at the studio?

"I will require three of them as personal assistants and I will provide you with a list of other needs. This will, of course, include an office here so that I may begin work on a script -- an opus that will forever throw this uncivilized world of barbarians into permanent shame for the travesty they have made out of this otherwise glorious natural planet."

J.B. and Puffy looked at each other in growing irritation and confusion. Puffy ventured:

"But ... ha hahaha ... maybe we ought to tone it down a little bit, Mr. Grump. I mean, if we tell 'em they're dung, they won't buy tickets. Gotta get the butts in the seats, you know. That's what makes the tinsel blow. Hahahaha.

"Is it just currency you're after then?" said Grump acidly. "The only thing that will help this miserable world is a manifesto so powerful and provocative and logical that all will have to take heed and repent from the silly idea of a God, that we're somehow divinely touched. We're all matter. Matter! Meat, actually, if you want to be cruel about it. Can't we see what is right before us? We will die! We are matter!"

"Wait a minute," shouted J.B. "Okay. That's it. You're not getting any of my money to make a movie. A little sex and violence. That's okay. But you can take that atheistic crap back to from where you came. Nobody's gonna pay to get dumped on. Who the hell are you to judge other people anyway?"

Grump stood up and spoke icily. "When will humans ever be able to face the truth? Can't you see all the things that are wrong with you?"

The tense scene is suddenly disturbed by the rapid step of a beautiful maid, with long, flowing blonde hair, a statuesque build, and carrying a silver tray and tea service.

The men watch admirably as she sits down the service before them and glides gracefully back out the door, hips undulating, disappearing.

Grump's eyes glazed, suddenly turned wilder in realization of something. "Who was that?" he asked urgently.

J.B. shrugged. "It wasn't Mrs. Watson. I think she's in the mail room. And we didn't order no tea."

Puffy walked to the door and looked outside, seeing nothing. They all stepped before the tea service and looked at its silvery glitter. Grump reached down and opened the server.

J.B. leaned over to sniff. The aroma of chamomile had a strangely relaxing effect, more relaxing than anything he had felt in years. It was a feeling of ... could it be .... peace? Nay! But still, he would have to practice this feeling. He breathed in more deeply.

There was a note on the tray. It said: Life is also like a can of salted nuts and a piece of sweet fruit."

"Of course!" exclaimed Grump. "This is an epiphany. It's not that life is all sugary like my dimwit brother once said. There is also salt! There is salt. There is also sugar. We are variously covered with each, and this is all ever-changing in our diets and lives. My salt is as sweet to me as my brother's simple sweetness ... which is, astoundingly, the same chocolate but covering many different combinations of things, raisins, nuts, toffees. We are each complex and simple in our ways. It is a truism ... a folk wisdom ... a philosophic gem to live through the ages. I shall make my own picture! It shall be a black comedy, at least a dingy gray."

"Sorry, Mr. Grump," groused J.B. "I'm shakin' my pants leg here. Better go shop that one to Miramax or some art house. In our shop, the axiom is: Simple Sells. Sex, violence, pretty people."

Grump broke out of his preoccupation. He stared at J.B. and then Puffy with disgust. "Can't you see, fools. This is a message from Forrest, my dearly estranged airheaded ... but lovable ... brother. He wants to make up. He knows I drink chamomile every night to wind down and sleep. He is telling me here to relax, that he understands me for the way I am, how I am, and wants to reconcile our differences. I'm off to Louisiana to the shrimp factory. Maybe we can work on a script together. He's just stupid enough to balance me out with Hollywood."

Grump stomped out of the room and down the hall. J.B. called after him, while Puffy perused the note.

"Don't call us, Grump. And we won't call you either. Ha! Hey, Puffy, this all gives me an idea ... long-lost twins, one good, one evil, thrown together by fate. And there's a girl. She has large breasts ..."

"Hey, look at this," said Puffy. "This is an advertising line for the new nuts and fruit store in the lobby. There's a note on the other side. It says: 'Free. One quarter-pound of fresh roasted peanuts on your first visit to our new store."

"Why do they send me tea?" asked J.B.

The door opened and the blonde beauty stepped in again. "I'm so sorry. This belongs in the other conference room. It's a special order for Mr. Nick Nolte. He's down the hall discussing a deal." She picks up the tray and whirls to leave.

"And what's this?" Puffy waves the note.

"Everybody in the building is getting them today. It's a new store in the lobby."

"Holy crap. What a misunderstanding we got going on," said Puffy. "Sure freaked out Grumpy Gus."

"Truth is," said J.B. "I just seen that this nut chain is now owned by Gump Enterprises. That's how they came up with the new tagline. Nuts for nuts, huh?"

Puffy just looked perplexed and pursed his lips. "Mmmmmm," he said. "Well ... anyways ... you was talkin' about twins with large breasts?

by Jim Cleveland

LIGHT EYES

May we always have our eyes on the light.

May we always be love-driven beacons

May we showcase that light in the love that is right

And join up with the heavenly legions.

May our lights join together on the path

Find our way in an aura of high reason

May we have the power in every waking hour

And feel love in every season.

IN SIGHT OF THE END

Tell me when we left that broad straight highway.
Tell me how we found this crooked trail.
We once thought our game was an expressway to fame.
Thought our lives would run true on that rail.
But now we see ditches left and right,
Spraying gravel, hurling rocks and spite
As we begin to see the end in sight.

Tell me where we spilled the elixir.
Liquid love a'flowing for the thrill.
We once drank so deep, now cautiously we creep
from place to place and scene to scene in our fears.
But now our days are only darkly bright,
In situations where we've hurt with psychic sleight
As we begin to see the end of all in sight.

Do you remember when we saw the first threads unravel
In this restless, loose-fit life of endless doubt.
We once wore fineries and reeked of cool
Weaving our experiences beyond all rules
But now our kites are torn without a flight
Grounded by the runway's flashing light
As we begin to see the end of all in sight.

I can face it now; it's clear to me
We won't be on this world forever, not meant to be.
But when we go, that's when we'll grow
into the love where we really want to be.
If the end is in sight, we know it'll be all right
Just let it be.
Let our souls be free.

by Jim Cleveland

REALIZED

As through this life I've traveled
By highway, air and sea
In all this time I've spent here
I found the best things are mine for free.
They are mirrored in my lover's eyes
Her beauty makes my feelings rise
When we're together, feels like forever
Sunset golden, purple heather
In the time that we're together
We are realized.

You can spend your money on pleasures
But they won't be your biggest treasures
You'll find that they're just measures
Of the Love that you can find.

You can travel to beautiful places
You can take in games and races
But they'll never match the graces
Of the Love that will some day be.

You can make yourself good friends
You can share with them from within
But it won't be that perfect Zen
Until that Lover comes along.

You can find some peace on earth
You can measure what you're worth
But to find that love light birth
The right one must come along.

I wish you well in the eternal quest
To find a Lover with a deep caress.
Lives to share, lives on the rise.
With two lives together, now realized.

Herding Those Cats

It's like herding cats, they say, implying that it is a frustratingly difficult challenge.

Indeed, the feline mind is individualistic and responds poorly to both pushing or pulling, yet it must have been that very challenge that motivated my great grandfather, who turned the herding of cats into a lucrative profession, for awhile anyway. He was always up for a difficult challenge.

Of course this was in the old country, and in a time where people lived quite differently than they do today.

Villages across the windy and cold countryside were invariably poor, the families scrapping for food among a few root crops and the mice of the field.

In time, however, as garbage dumps in the villages grew larger, they attracted many more mice, and they soon grew into rats. And so the villagers were able to turn their refuse piles into a source of food, meat, protein. Soon every man in the villages were commonly seen with long rat-killing pipes strapped to their waist and legs. The clubs became known as 'ratatouilles' or rat tools and they were quite effective against pudgy rodents sated with beet and turnip greens and defecation. Later, a stew-like dish became known as ratatouille as well.

This food chain worked well for a few years and the diet of the villagers was improved. But soon, wild and resourceful predators showed up -- fierce cats who began to harvest the rodents and drive the villagers, with their swinging cudgels, from the feeding fields.

In truth, these ferocious, sharp-clawed cats were the embittered ancestors of a time when the village did have a few house cats as pets. But when the people began eating the cats, there was panic and only a few cats managed to escape into the wilds, where they began breeding on their own and living, no doubt, embittered lives.

And now these cats had returned, direly threatening the rat food supply. The villages first tried withholding the garbage, but to no avail. The rats soon dug underground and made elaborate tunnels to evade the cats, riddling the landscape with a subterranean culture that the villages soon began to call Rodentia. Cats began to invade the villages and break into dwellings in search of rodents that might be harbored, and even secretly bred, by the citizens.

Into this war scene stepped my great grandfather, a successful businessman and the inventor of the spray bottle, which had pumped new vigor into seltzer water sales from coast to coast. He saw both a business opportunity and a way to refute the folk legend about cat herding difficulties.

If he could actually herd cats successfully, and replicate the system in any village, then his fortune would be made.

by Jim Cleveland

The village of Buttchiques was the first to contract with my esteemed ancestor, and soon he arrived to address city hall flanked by a team of workers in leather body suits and armed with a belt of seltzer spray bottles, containing a variety of attack liquids. They wore heavy boots with spikes protruding from the toes.

An elaborate geographical and architectural plan was hatched and on the prescribed day of attack, a solid line of human operatives in full leather, spray bottles at the ready began marching down off the hills surrounding the villages, a wave of cats reluctantly going before them, angry but giving ground readily to the barrage of spritzer bottles.

Down across the garbage land they ran, the spraying mass of humanity pressing them on steadily, crunching their boots through the mushy pile and spurting water spray as their vanguard. Cats hated water and my great grandfather knew how to make the most of it.

Into the village they ran, past all the securely locked doors and windows, scrambling across the cobblestone streets in a screeching, meowing mass of aqua-induced discontent.

There was a park full of trees on the waterfront, but they provided no refuge. Some in the squalling cat mass tried to climb the trunks or leap onto the low-lying limbs but my great grandfather was way ahead of them. Armed men were stationed in the trees and fiercely sprayed down the cats, which fell back into the mass, and it roiled raucously on toward the water.

But driving hundreds of wild cats into the water was, of course not realistic, and not part of this splendid plan. A brick wall some 500 feet long had been constructed there on the coastline and the cats were driven straight into it, eventually to the center where a wide portal, a tunnel in the wall, was the only means of escape.

And so the cats ran headlong through the portal and into the dark tunnel that led outside and starkly to the ocean cliff. There they crashed in huge numbers off the cliff and onto the unforgiving rocks below. Many cats perished. Those few that survived were washed out to sea or else battled down favorable currents to an island several miles away.

The operation was a triumph and my great grandfather had launched a service business for the entire country. It would be coupled with a big upturn in seltzer bottle sales, and all was well. The high protein rat diet was restored while providing a productive means of waste disposal. It was a win-win.

My ancestor was deemed a 'catter' and that was how those in the new cat herding profession would be known. The wall in Buttchiques was known, historically, as the Catter Wall. Others would follow up and down the country. When there was no rocky coastline to send the spritzer-driven felines, huge pits were constructed on the other side, where the fleeing cats would fall into electrified water pits. Their shocking conclusions would provide yet another protein source for the village. My great grandfather would parlay this new technology into yet another successful business in electrical cattle prods.

But then it all changed. Somehow a contaminant was introduced to the food supply. While the rats seemed unaffected, a horrible plague swept across Buttchiques and other villages. A mysterious ailment was killing people and yet the rodent food supply was unaffected -- very perverse. How could this be?

Finally, the villagers had mostly died, but a few over 50 bedraggled survivors made their way down the coastline, and were soon seeking refuge on a small island just off the coast, to where they could wade. Perhaps being off the shore would be some protection against the ravaging disease.

Alas, they were met strongly at the beach by a herd of wild cats. There they were, ferocious survivors of my great grandfather's elaborate panacea to the village they had imperiled. Whether the creatures consciously hated the humans is a matter of speculation, but they had no intention to share the island and were at the ready with fangs and claws and bristling back hairs.

The desperate and unarmed surviving humans would be no match for the wild cats, for sure, and so they tried a gesture of feigned friendship. Some had brought along dead rats and now they offered them to the cats that were commanding the shoreline. It seemed that the gesture of friendship might actually work, but in the short term, the cats ate the bounty and still disdained the humans and drove them back into the shallow water to take their case elsewhere, back to the mainland.

Soon, however, all of the cats died of the plague. The humans were huddled on the mainland beach in a cluster of shacks and they found a new diet there, of crabs and fish and shrimp. They developed a new way of living and of eating.

One day, they sent a pair of men back to the island, only to find all of the cats dead and gone. The area was littered with rotting corpses and skeletons. What could possibly have killed them? The surviving humans were wondering what it was that they couldn't see. It had to be a curse of some kind. Why? Because curses could not be seen. No one had ever seen one. They were not material. It had to be a curse.

They had actually tried to help the island cats, having sacrificed the rat protein they had taken to eat along the trail to placate them, and perhaps make them more docile. Whatever had befallen the cats, at least they were not to blame. In fact, they could have co-existed with the cats, the humans thought now, unless they would sometime be needed again for the food supply. Anyway, they inherited the island.

Above all, the humans knew now that they must be constantly vigil that future garbage piles not be contaminated with whatever it was that contaminated the one in their old village. As the village grew again, one of its top priorities was to build a large fence around its garbage dump so that this unknown menace might be kept out and not poison their rodent food supply.

While they could not realistically build a new rat population unless there was food, my great grandfather was able to help again, by selling the village electrified fencing. In the morning, it became a gratifying ritual for villagers to walk the fence and collect a variety of already partially cooked and hair seared carcasses -- a ready source of protein without endangering the village's garbage resources, which were only being used as a lure now, and not open to some contaminant as it would be on unfenced property.

And then my great grandfather intervened again. Now retired and an Extinguished Fellow at the Global Critter Institute, he had long taken an interest in Buttchiques, that being the location of his breakout fame. It was to his lament that the deserted village and his vine-en-shrouded Catter Wall were all that was left of this once redeemed village.

Together with other professors, he now visited the survivors of Buttchiques downstream, on a small island they now called Catskills, commemorating the mass die-off of the felines there. The people were told now that new scientific findings were indicating that the garbage pile itself would be inherently contaminated, with an invisible curse upon it. It was now speculated that the Great Source above had made this so in order that man be implored to bury or burn this kind of refuse and not have such dumps sully the beautiful landscape of the Divine Creation.

Science now also indicated that the rats were polluted by the curse of the garbage and spread that curse, which erupted in disease, to all of the village. That explained why people who had not been to the garbage dump at all took ill and died with the others. The curse used the rats in a kind of ironic vengeance, a blessing of protein wrapped into a killing curse that they brought into the homes. Such irony.

Soon, the new village was burying its garbage and killing all rats and mice on sight, while enjoying a new seafood diet that made everyone more healthy. It was discovered that cats are strongly attracted to a seafood diet and so a few wild survivors began to hang around, beg for food and become domesticated. And so, eventually, most homes had a loving cat and they had seafood feasts in the evenings together with the family. Kids played with the fish-sated felines and all was well.

Meantime, my great granddad parlayed new knowledge into yet another new business. He turned fish scraps into cat food and sold it in cans. For the labor required, he was able to send a ship to Ireland, where the potato famine had made many destitute. These workers were carried across the sea to establish new villages and work in the cat food plant.

Soon, they were to be known as the Meow Micks, immigrant workers launching this new business which would bring additional investment into the area. Later, this slang name became an actual brand name for the company, as did Nien Lives, named after the island of Nien, where the resurrected human village first found life when the cats had all mysteriously died after being driven from the old village and colonizing there.

My great granddad also had his famous Catter Wall monument removed from the old village site and transported brick by brick to the island. To entertain visitors to the island, he soon installed pegs into the wall and founded a lucrative new business. He combined the walls and pegs with a harness operation on a wire and turned it into a successful amusement feature, soon marketing it to theme parks across the world as a challenging climbing experience with either triumph at the top or an exhilarating swing at the finish.

By now, of course, the catter business was completely gone. There was no reason to herd cats any more and they mostly lived in separate households, having humans to feed and clean up after them for all of their lives.

Lacking both cats and rats as food sources, the villagers built fishing craft and set sail to harvest more and more seafood, which had become the diet staple, and a source of food for the pet cats as well.

My great granddad, very aged by now, still had the savvy to develop another business in his last years, powerfully strong fishing nets developed from catgut, a product of the Critter Institute laboratories. This required some inter-breeding among known cat species in order that the gut itself be exceptionally strong. These cats were named fittingly after my great granddad, whose name was Alexander Lee, but referred to by all of his friends as simply Al Lee.

In time, the famous Al Lee cats, as they were known, were recognized as the most rugged and hearty breed one could own. Their gut strength was extraordinary.

In Mr. Lee's golden years, research was being concentrated on reducing cat food costs by setting up a system wherein they eat human garbage. Rats, naturally attracted to garbage, would be electrocuted by hidden implants inside the garbage piles and their carcasses would provide ever more food for the cats. The cats would be nurtured on garbage and dead rodents at hardly any cost at all, except for the electrical charges from my great grandfather's utility company, which had grown out of the electrical cattle prod business.

It seemed to be a good plan. Mice consume waste and become rats wherein they are executed by electrical charges embedded within the heap, in order become placid food for mild-mannered domesticated house cats who could simply be free to forage. They wouldn't have to be fed nearly as much canned food any more and the one-two electro-cat strategy would keep communities clean from the cursed garbage.

But times had changed. People now feared garbage piles as inherently contaminated and cursed and believed that the rodents carried that curse out to the people, and they might get sick and die as had their ancestors in the plague years. Society began to burn garbage in big smoking incinerators where the poison was pushed up into the sky. Or they dumped it at sea so that it could dissolve in water. Rats were despised now, and killed at every opportunity in an effort at total eradication. And cats, whom people agreed had a lovely appearance and a comforting presence, invariably dined on commercial products at varying levels of quality in a tiered market. With the knowledge that their cat food sales would also be cannibalized, the idea was dropped. Garbage food was simply out of style.

How times had changed on that day that Mr. Lee passed peacefully during his afternoon nap, a pedigreed and very fat Al Lee cat snuggling in his lap and one of his signature spritzer bottles by the chair.

The cat had inexplicably taken to getting into the kitchen garbage pail for scraps and Mr. Lee had resorted to spraying water in his face to discourage the behavior. He had worried that the cat might pick up a germ. There was this very new concept that tiny, invisible curses called 'germs' were everywhere around us, little teeny bits of unseen near nothing that would make us sick. It seemed far-fetched, but still possible.

My great grandfather had seen many changes during his lifetime, from a young and wild catter subduing the feline population to the developer and nurturer of a new wave of domestic felines named for him that now served the pet needs of countless citizens of his country. Where once he worked to destroy these animals he had come to breed and feed them and furnish them to captive and captivated households nationwide.

In the end, it was a victory for the cat kingdom, which no longer had to forage in garbage to eat, but were still free for recreational grazing as they wished. The docile and doting humans were responsible almost completely for their upkeep.

People even laugh these days that you can't herd cats. They're going to do what they want. Hahaha.

But I have read the family history and I know better. And I learned a few lessons as well.

My company now has access to seven African countries where my team of operatives fly into controlled zones and corral lions and other wild cats for the zoo trade. They use a new generation of electrical prod and fencing technology, excellent catgut netting and spritzer-delivered cat food laced with sleep inducing chemicals . Cats are herded to a wall constructed of compacted catnip. An animalistic version of Ambien is simultaneously sprayed from planes overhead. Within an hour, my company can load up a dozen or more cats and we fly them to zoos all across the country.

It's not only possible to herd cats but under the right circumstances it can be profitable as well.

PART TWO

ABSURDLY SIMPLE SPIRITUALITY

21 SPIRITUAL EMPOWERMENTS FOR THE 21st CENTURY

Workshop at the Teaching Mission Universal Gathering,
Park City, Utah; July 5-9, 2001

Good afternoon. I welcome you to a workshop that will be both analytical and experiential. Together we will cover 21 new age spiritual axioms that you can learn, know, and apply to enhance your spiritual growth in these times of great - and quickening - revelation. The Urantia Book, which we study, says our planet is "quivering on the brink ..."

The brink of what?

Profound spiritual opportunities. Powerful spiritual energies to access. These empowerments will help you get beyond the need for human gurus, for human teachers, for human methods.

Knowledge is power - when it is applied to action. Faith and Love are wonderful for example. But so much more wonderful when applied to Service.

My associate presenters today will be:

The OneTeam. This is a collective of celestial teachers who speak with one voice - the Melchizedek curriculum, along with their own personal perceptions relating to this curriculum. This team and I have co-created a manuscript called "Beyond Cynicism: Liberating Voices from the Spirit Within." Cynical questions about the madness of the world; loving answers that touch the heart and expand our perceptions.

Also helping will be the **Celestial Artisans.** They are ready to help you too. Just call on Bakim at any time and ask for artistic inspiration to represent spiritual values.

Also helping will be **Van Morrison.** Hope some of you have some Irish soul. We will have three songs designed to assist you in the feeling of Beingness ... in visualization ... and to immerse yourself in an auditory experience ... and to glean from them three of the 21 spiritual empowerments we will discuss. Van expresses them better than I can.

We will need to THINK, and we will need to release ourselves from thinking during this time. We will fuse the intellectual and analytical with the intuitive feelingness, knowingness, beingness ... while utilizing the mind, body and spirit.

The Empowerments are stacked here ... and ready (a stack of paper).

So let's first move into an experience that provides a vibratory framework with which to review 21 spiritual empowerments for the 21st century.

Let's begin with a little analysis. Let's say you are saying that you wonder if the premise for this workshop is absurd. When is it that we don't need gurus, teachers, a master plan, for ourselves and the universe? Has there ever been such a time? Will there be?

Well, I'm sure you already know, or you wouldn't be here, that there are times we can get beyond the need for instruction. Special moments when we feel the power of God's energies in a great Beingness, Feelingness and Knowingness.

(Relaxation, Centering Exercise) Let us relax now and prepare to receive an experience in sound and visualization ... and strong clues to several of our 21 spiritual empowerments ...

Experience this ... *(Music: No Guru, No Method, No Teacher)*

Are we wet with the rain of the Holy Spirit?

What do we glean from Van Morrison's magical moment that he crystallized into a magnificent musical expression? It will be a recurring question with more than one answer.

When you are immersed in a moment's beautiful vision, a special feeling, a loving heart, you don't need a guru to tell you about God. You don't need a teacher to teach you about God. You don't need a method to approach the issue of God. Meeting God in the moment is a matter of ... not trying in any way but ... Release to the Holy Spirit ... no plan, no agenda, no method. God is here. Mother Spirit is here. Jesus is here. It is a garden of sensuous ... soulful ... spiritualizing delight.

If we are now wet with rain and shivering in expectation, we can sit relaxed and begin to open the pages of spiritual empowerment for our brand new century. They are here ... and they are nuggets of wisdom that can empower you as apostles of light, missionaries of Truth, Beauty and Goodness.

Spiritual Empowerment No. 1

GOD IS WITH YOU AND IN YOU.
GOD SEES YOU AS YOU.
EVERY SECOND TRUE.

This is something everyone should know. Knowledge of this is empowering.

No matter your environment, from the gardens to the ghettoes, your Heavenly Universal Father experiences this life with you.

This is a transmission from the OneTeam for you:

"Within you there is the pilot house of God. Hard. Strongly built like bricks and mortar. A beacon of light encased to show you the way to daily feelings of peace and comfort. To bring your ship to ports of call in your growth plan, a plan as unique as your indwelling spirit which strives to fuse with your personality into a higher being, ever closer to God.

"Accept your childhood of God, in your glorious imperfections, glorious because they are part of the Grand Plan of all the Universes. Bringing you to perfection. Feel God inside you each day, each moment, each second, from the knowingness of this magnificent cosmology. The Fifth Epochal Revelation is given to you with all the joyous best wishes of the Universe and its multitude of peaceful, God-knowing and loving inhabitants. Beyond this, behold many more beautiful and insightful expressions of this new age, including your own."

My take on this:

Well ... We, in this room, know well the Fifth Epochal Revelation and so we are already empowered with this knowledge coming into this today. We know about the Thought Adjuster by whatever name and can more precisely define this presence than most people. But this is great news indeed for a lot of our fellow Urantians.

Spiritual Empowerment No. 2

ASCENSION IS THE ONLY PLAN ... THE ONLY RACE WE EVER RAN

Yes, we just mentioned ascension, as opposed to revisionist ideas such as ... reincarnation. If humankind can't imagine Mansion Worlds and can't explain Deja Vu, they might get some supposedly inspired advice that we just keep coming back here – recycling until we get it right. These ancient seers might not have the knowledge and conviction that there are millions of planets and trillions of beings. In fact, some supposedly smart people are still asking in 2001: Is there life on other planets? Some are still saying that Earthlings are God's chosen people. Some still say if we kick a dog, we will likely be reincarnated as one.

I think our imaginations have always gotten carried away in the interest of making a good story. And some wise seers have come to think that their every thought and dream was inspired.

Ascension. It is a plan that honors you wherever you are on the path, even if you get off the path and wind up in a briar thicket. No matter if you stop and sit down on a stump ..... of a tree you foolishly chopped down.

Ascension is the plan. Grow your soul. Create the Supreme with the mighty tools of worship, prayer, forgiveness and service.

This, indeed, is information people should know. In this room, you already know it. Congratulations. We will get you some fresh stuff in a moment.

Here's my transmission from the OneTeam:

"There are many ways to learn without retarding growth. There are many ways to ascend without starting over. Memories are tools that are not often trashed."

Why don't we learn that we build from where we are? We move forward from wherever we are on the path. Why erase memory and start over? Life isn't a board game. We don't have to experience life as a blind beggar to know that life poignantly, from the empathy and love we can feel in the moment ... just like in a beautiful garden seeing a beautiful girl and feeling the sweet dampness in the gentle air.

We should be thinking newness and ascension, not recyclement into an evolving world because it is the only one we know and can imagine. And karma works very well without reincarnation. And reincarnation works very well too ... on Mansonia.

Spiritual Empowerment No. 3

THE STILLNESS FOR ENERGY AND SYNERGY FOR YOU ... THROUGH AND THROUGH

We are energized in the Stillness. We know this too, after hearing the teachers talk about it and lead us into it for some 10 years now. It is, of course, an empowerment.

In this ritual of relaxation and open faith, in the quietness from distractions, with a mind as an open canvas, asking God's blessings, into worship, prayer, forgiveness and voicing the words of celestial teachers through the enhanced energy circuitry ... we gain spiritual empowerment every day.

We go forward in greater balance, in greater peace and surety, and inspired by the energies that come through only through this special time. It is like pulling into the gas station for some high octane.

From the Celestial Artisans:
The Stillness is an oasis of spring
That tingles your spirit to smiling
Enthralls with nuggets of gleaming insight
You call forth in joyous admiring.

And each little nugget that passes your fingers
Is such a pure and genuine article
Sparkling in sunlight, glistening clingers
That make up each memorable particle

Spend some time with the Father each day. Father has met you more than halfway. Living inside you, experiencing life with you, assuring you salvation if you will make the effort toward your own salvation by .... spreading Love. If we do this, that's enough.

And we will be empowered.

Spiritual Empowerment No. 4

SPIRITUALIZE THE SECONDS, MEMORIALIZE THE MOMENTS,
HARMONIZE THE HOURS IN GOODNESS AND YOU

In keeping with all this, you soon learn that you can take the Stillness with you as you live your day. You can bring it into you in spare moments as you ease yourself into feelings of worshipful gratitude and looking for ways to spread some kindness with the next person you meet.

Take a moment, center yourself. Ask for love and empowerment and promise to share it with the next person you meet. A moment or two is enough to find and reaffirm your ... Center.

Then go into service. Sometimes just a smile is a powerful thing. Do it with waitresses and garbage collectors and clerks and panhandlers. And for those last folks, maybe give them 50 cents too. Tell them God loves them.

Spiritual Empowerment No. 5

ENTHRALL WITH ART ... YOURSELF AND APART.

Enthrall yourself with art. Enthrall others as you can. As you can express yourself more fully.

I listened to our feature song and went into the mystic and sat down to be blessed by the celestial artisans once again. In a stream, they sent me:

> *Who could want more in life than the heartfelt instances of*
> *Beingness with God*
> *in a garden wet with rain*
> *in songs so sweet through sweeter refrains*
> *and in silence glorious where peace can reign*
> *upon this celestial plain*
>
> *As silver streaks, I imagine angels in the skyscapes above my head,*
> *Closer to God*
> *in fluffy clouds of wet and blue*
> *softly expressing, embracing, imbued*
> *within our soulful waftings so free and so true*
> *reflecting this wondrous hue*

As stillness energies permeate our circle and bring feelings of
Experiencing God
we sit softly, quietly in askance of grace
that holy spirit will wash over this place
and bring us together in glorious embrace
leaving the mundane and that forsaken race
to stand in this garden and look into your face.
Wet with rain.

No Guru, No Method, No Teacher
Just this eternal moment with the Father – Mind
Just this powerful empathy with Jesus – Body
Just this energizing embracing with the Mother – Spirit
Just this Holy Sonship with All Go
that you know in the moment to be true.
Feeling and experiencing the knowingness of children
of the universe school.

I believe that's us.

Each and every one of us in this room is … Creative. The Universe of Universes is all about … Creation. Humankind and celestials create in many ways with many instruments. The celestial artisans have more than we, more senses, more colors, higher conceptual under-standings. Here as mere mortals, we are lucky to start at the beginning so we can taste it all throughout our Ascension, including the Arts.

We will learn our own instruments and stretch them to their limits and beyond and create new boundaries that will be surpassed by our children's children's children. We will be given more instruments of art on Mansonia. Each one a joyous gift in our ascension, a fresh new step, a new instrument on the path to our misssion goal: "Be Ye Perfect."

And hopefully make good art along the way. Art is empowering. And we will eventually become perfect artists too.

Learn to use your creative tools. Create for yourself a balanced personality, who glides in the walk, captures the moment, brightens rooms with laughter and love. Painters and plumbers both have their creative tools. And athletes and actors and archaeologists and archers …. and all of us.

From the OneTeam:

"In finding creative expressions in their life, God-centered humans do much to further their morontial development. Occupying one's mind and body and spirit in the quest of creating

something of lasting value that one hopes will be appreciated by others is a high calling. And as the person is occupied thusly, there is the absence of the dawdling, self-effacing insecurity that forever threatens this evolutionary quest.

Go beyond your fears, and the Universal Father will be pleased with the strength that is help-ing to bring forward the great Creation – the one in which you now, in your time, can gently or profoundly assist."

Spiritual Empowerment 6:

THE ENERGY IS IN PLACE ... ACCESS IT WITH FAITH

Here's one you know too:

Celestial teachers, guides and angels are everywhere, seeking to make contact with us and help our spiritual growth. They are here in greater numbers now because of the opening of spiritual energy circuits in recent years.

So the Teaching Mission is in place. And many other bold and adventurous spiritual outreach programs across the planet. They are here for you. Explore them and test them through the Spirit of Truth that Jesus left for you. The Urantia Book tells us to find the com-monalities, not the differences.

Taste the excitement of the Pleiadians and the Course in Miracles, the Ascended Masters and Tantra Yoga, sacred sex, and the Pentecostals and the Christian Revivalists and the Buddhist world and the Monks at Gethsemani and the Ravers and the Wiccans and ... gosh, well ... maybe even the Southern Baptists.

Explore the spiritual universe. It is here for you. Don't be afraid. Jesus did it; he traveled broadly, he studied, he shared, and he loved everyone he ever met ... and he loves everyone who ever lived ... and who will ever live in the future live because of his own magnificent creation ... steeped like no other in mercy and compassion and forgiveness from the events that happened here. Explore the World of the Cross. It is like no other.

A quicker way to say this is that ... energy circuitry is being opened incrementally. There is a spiritual renaissance well underway ... a correcting time for past errors and defaults ... a time of burgeoning, more readily accessible spiritual energies that we can access via the spiritual stillness.

And you do not ... you do not need other people to tap into them for you. And you don't need to go to the Pyramids and stand on some vortex ... unless you want to. Sounds like fun to me, but the energy is everywhere and within you as well.

You can talk to God at your kitchen table. Because God is there with you.

Spiritual Empowerment 7:

YOUR WILL IS FREE ... LIKE IT OR NOT

Our free wills are always in charge in this evolutionary world. A vital difference between TR and trance channeling is that the human transmitter is in a state of relative consciousness, choosing cooperatively to work with the celestial teacher. Choosing to say the next word or not. A vessel for the tonal flow.

Not that there is anything wrong with trance channeling, by the way. There is a body of channeled work through the decades that is worth reading and considering. But they are archival, prelude to today, in 2001, when energies are higher and humankind is ready for enhanced revelation. For current information, you are perfectly capable of transmitting material that reflects modern times and is tailored specifically for you.

And with all of this, your free will is sacred. You always make the decision of what you think, what you say and what you do. Trance channels are faced with the very same responsibility when they wake up from momentary service.

I know that some will tell you that you must surrender your will to God. God doesn't want it. He gave it to you. It is a gift. Use it. And don't complain because it brings with it great responsibilities. Those are gifts too.

From the artisans:
Urantia is a school for material experiences,
walking the walk and keeping appearances,
and finding a way to get over the humps
and laugh and have faith when you feel all the bumps.
Urantia is a world full of markdowns and clearances
that we walk in our faith and our Father's assurances.
And it is yours. You are welcome.

God respects your free will so much that it is never violated.

The Ancients of Days will settle up with you on down the trail, after all. And will settle up as well with all the evil tyrants who have spread death and suffering.

Spiritual Empowerment 8:

IN GOD, FAILURE IS NOT AN OPTION

Well, I know most of you knew this one already. We did get through the rollover of the century on the manmade clock, of course – both of them, actually, depending on whether you like straight math or apocalyptic math. And whether you accept the very first year as Zero. Talk about starting on the bottom. You have to start at 0 and work 12 months to even get up to 1.

So here it is in a nutshell.

The earth is not headed toward catastrophic or apocalyptic doom. The love energy that we generate and the actual service that we perform, combined with expanding celestial insights and inspiration, will help lift the world to a higher level of spiritual consciousness. This is a very special place -- the planet of Jesus' incarnation. We can help create a glorious destiny for the family of Man.

Now, I know some folks who say that mass destruction is the best lesson you can learn. We screw up the environment, we choke to death. We squander our fossil fuel while falling way behind on fossil manufacturing.

I don't know about that. I think we can reap a bitter harvest for what we have sowed. And we will and are. But I believe we can learn a lot more by Redemption than by failure ... meeting the challenges head-on and with the benevolent power of the entire Celestial Administration working with us.

We will learn much more by saving the world than by losing it.

And I believe that God wants us to learn the greater lesson of redemption, not failure. The assurance of salvation through faith and love and service. There can be nothing more powerful than faithful, loving service, so I don't see any kind of failure possible.

Spiritual Empowerment 9:

THE HEALING HAS BEGUN

Yes, it has. People need to know this. It will empower them to be open to new gifts of the spirit. Not many years ago, you could smoke anywhere.

Not many years ago, people thought cannabis would make you goofy and lazy.

Not many years ago, the allopathic medical profession with its powerful pharmaceutical and insurance triad reigning supreme, dominated the health care scene. Now, holistic prevention and healing practices have captured a major share of the market. They help with age-old problems like colds and flu and backaches and arthritis, stress and anxiety and uneasiness and on and on that doctors haven't been able to defeat with their get sick-get help plan.

Healthy lifestyles are coming on strong. Herbals will balance and invigorate. Colors and tones and touch and energetic loving vibrations are part of a new Healing Age. It is coming. It is well on the way.

Today, hospitals take out full page Sunday paper ads touting new wellness centers with therapies that they once disdained as quackery. Doctors are talking about the power of prayer and angels coming to help with mortal transitions.

The healing has begun. Be part of it. For you and others. Heal others and be healed in the sharing of your vibrant energies.

Spiritual Empowerment 10:

EMPATHY EMPOWERS

Go ahead. Be weak. Shed some tears. Hurt inside when your loved ones hurt. It is empowering. It shows your strengths of the spirit.

It flows your spirit of love to the universe, and across a planet known for the special empathetic characteristics of our Creator Son, Michael, Jesus – mercy, forgiveness, compassion, respect for all of living creation. Hallmarks of our special planet…. a legacy you can aspire to.

Jesus' mission as the Son of Man was a consummately powerful adventure in universal empathy. He was empowered by it. Humankind was empowered by it. The local universe and the superuniverse were empowered by it. You can be empowered by it too.

Empower your Essence with Empathy.

Spiritual Empowerment 11:

PURITY IS REALITY

The Urantia Book tells us that we see life as darkness with small patches of light. In truth, it is lightness with patches of dark.

(Demonstration with white, clean sheet of paper. Besmirch with black marker here and there, but our essence is light. Crumple paper and throw away, our lives end. Another white sheet of paper symbolizes a new life, an innocent and pure babe, born of hope.)

From the Celestial Artisans:

> *Your latitude is seen in your attitude*
> *Which lives beneath your platitudes*
> *You can choose to see light*
> *Or you can choose dark*
> *You can make life a jungle*
> *Or work on a park.*

Spiritual Empowerment 12:

Here's one I'll bet you forgot. You used to have it; am not sure you still do. Van has to travel to Ireland and go back in time for it.

(Song: A Sense of Wonder)

So number 12 is:

BE A CHILD IN WONDER

Don't lose the Wonder of the Creation. The marvels of Earth from ants to mountains, from seas to starfields, from butterflies to books to wedding bells.

Treasure your good memories. Store them and share them. And don't lose the innocent sense of wonder of it all ... of being a child ... a child of God ... a child of the creation .... a child of our society that we would build in love ... a child of the universe. Love yourself as a child. Be as loving as a child. Be wet with rain in the garden ... and it will help you grow.

> *"And then one day, you came back home.*
> *You were a creature all enraptured.*
> *You had the key to your soul.*
> *and you did open, that day you came back*
> *To the Garden."*

Have a sense of wonder. Apply it to every passing moment as you walk with God. Worship the Universal Father by fully appreciating all our bountiful gifts and finding new ones as we grow.

Spiritual Empowerment 13:

IT'S NOT WHAT YOU BELIEVE, IT'S HOW YOU BELIEVE

Well, you know the Bible is full of errors and even embarrassments. But it has saved many a soul. And it will save many more because it is the "Word." Whose word? The word of the people who wrote the chapters. What did they know about spiritual realities? Not much. A great deal of the Bible's most beautiful and inspiring material was taken from older texts.

But no matter. If people want to deify their scriptures ... if people want to worship the Sun God ... if people think it's wrong to have a beer ... True Religion is a personal experience anyway.

Believe what you want. Just love another. Love one another. That's all the aged and frail John had to say when they helped him to the pulpit in his twilight days. He had encapsulated it all: "Brothers and sisters, Love one another." That says it all.

It's how you believe. Do you represent spiritual values? Do you walk the walk? This is our daily challenge. It doesn't matter what you think about reincarnation or Republicans.

Spiritual Empowerment 14:

DON'T DUMP ON DOGMA. IT'S OKAY IF IT WORKS

Some of us have wanted to do battle with Fundamentalists in the past. It's time to give them a break.

Yes, sometimes they are exclusive and quick to condemn other people to some place called Hell. People like Dante and various deluded religonists developed this whole mythology of damnation and hellfire and used it to control the minds and the tithes of the people.

Okay, let's let bygones be bygones. That's hot lava under the bridge. It dilutes energy to go to war with fundamentalists.

Christ Michael once transmitted a beautifully succinct message to those who would antagonize the fundamentalists. "Don't disturb my sheep."

We are in Michael's flock. They are too. Let's go through life with humility and grace and be an inspiration to all those in our aura. Cast an aura of loving light.

And know that the fundamentalists have the same opportunities in the Ascension plan as we do.

If we spend our time fighting fundamentalists, it will retard the positive energies we could be vibrating instead.

If debate is ever called for in the need for education and enlightenment, do it in the spirit of love. Perhaps you are being called to spread truer spiritual values in a confrontational framework. Fine. Do so as an opportunity to respond as Jesus would. And thus, you will grow from it. And surely, so will your audience.

Spiritual Empowerment 15:

DON'T COMPLAIN ... IT SPREADS THE PAIN

How many go through life in constant complaining. It's the coffee shop ritual. It's the voice of frustration that things don't always go right. It's feeling the pangs of our imperfections.

Well ... let's get real. These are the Time and Space Worlds. This ain't supposed to be perfect. The point is to work on it. Together. And we've made our own beds here collectively and often singularly. So get over it and get on with it.

If each of us could make a solemn promise to just go through one week, starting Sunday morning maybe, without registering complaints in our speech, it might make a great difference in our lives. At the end of one week of conscious effort to express only positive thoughts, we might well see a big change happen with our permanent attitude, and thereby a big change in our lives.

From the artisans:

Show your light. It's all right
The Father's gift to break the night.
It's holy pure the way you smile
when it's real just like a child
Show your light. It's all right
Be a child and make it bright.

Show your light. It wants to grow
The Father's gift that makes you flow
with beauty real just like a child
yet knowing great truths all the while
Show your light. Make it glow
A happy child in sparkling snow.

Show your light. Make it sharing
The Father's gift through you in caring
Holy pure in the way you give it
In every passing day and minute
Show your light. Vibrate it right
And be a child with us tonight.

Well, I don't see anything about complaining in there .... typically they ignore such trivialities and move forward to advance the energy, in the way we felt it as an innocent child but in knowing the truths all the while.

Spiritual Empowerment 16:

SELFLESS SERVICE SERVES US SURELY

Did you ever get loaded on illegal substances back in the 60s or 70s and try to say those alliterated phrases fast ... like

Six Sicilian Sailors Sailing the Seven Seas.

How about: Nine Nubile Nubians Nibbling Nougats, Nuggets and Nicotine.

This karmic insight needs no alliteration ... and you know it too. Every step in faith is rewarded. Every kindness comes back to us. Every act of love is rewarded. It is a Law of Reciprocity.

You don't do kind things in the hope of reward. But as you are rewarded and blessed, you grow in faith and love and desire to live Truth and Beauty and Goodness and do all the kind things you can. Giving and receiving Love is the currency of the Universe.

From the One Team:
"To be selfless is to recognize the transient purpose of our mortal selves and the eternal truth of reciprocal, all empowering love. Instead, be self-full, full of the holy spirit that brings you the ultimate reality on the mortal plain, and look with anticipation upon the flowering of an even fuller and more beautiful self as you traverse the plateaus of your ascension."

And the artisans: *Live in love each step you take*
and you will find the garden gate
where love grows full and blooms inside
and takes your hand to be your guide
and love will always guide you true
in every day, in all you do
to find the fragrance of all that's self
blossomed wide to a nobler quest.
To know the Perfect Love held forth
you will reach it one day, of course.

Spiritual Empowerment 17:

ATTUNE THE TONES:... ACCESS THE POWER OF MUSIC

Music is far more than entertainment ... background for K-Mart Shoppers ... a way to shriek your frustrations to a mosh-pit of lost children. There are healing and attunement powers within music that you are just beginning to consider and learn about and access. Utilize it to open conduits to the world of Beauty and sensitivity. Development of the senses.

Be attuned to the new knowledge. Be prepared to find the perfect adjustments to give you peaceful bliss and an open threshold to spiritual inspiration. The circuits are re-opening, incrementally as we can assimilate greater revelations of truth, beauty and goodness. We are helping bring forth these energies co-creatively with the celestials, through our words and deeds on Urantia.

Be sure to explore all the rich textures and tones of world music, new age music. Increasingly, music will pull the world's peoples together. Recognize its power and access it. Find the tones that resonate positively.

Spiritual Empowerment 18:

COME TO YOUR SENSES; ENHANCE WITH ROMANCE

Seeing, Hearing, Touching, Smelling, Tasting. Do we appreciate these great gifts? They are more than perfunctory, rudimentary, scaffolds to something better. They are loving endowments to mortals like us. Do we use them well? Create treats for them and share them with others?

How can we be empowered with more and greater senses when we haven't learned to master and magnify the ones we have? Have we learned to work with all of them harmoniously and fruitfully? Have we learned how to share them fully with intimate and empowering partners in order to reach higher levels of vibration? Are we artists in our senses - culinary chefs, passionate lovers, speakers of beautiful words, listeners to the inner voice.

We need to come to our senses and work on this.

Our sensory experiences are often ...Enhanced with Romance. Here is a narrative from Darien, a celestial artisan.

LIVING MOMENTS

Morning broke gently in glistening spikes
of radiance and resonance, oncoming light,
that flooded her doorstep down through the pines
to the banks of the lake where spirit light shines
in sparkles and speckles and seamless design,
rays that go dancing altogether in time.

LIVING MOMENTS
(cont.)

This love scene it opens her soul-searching day.
She sits on the deck in the morning wash phase
The coffee smoke trickles up in vaporous climb
to melt in the fabric of this airy design
that wafts out its fragrances, each one in its time,
in-mingling the day's energizing sunshine.

She sat in its aura and breathed in so fine,
and felt the light's warmness, felt God's love inside,
as the day turned to noontime and the late day sublime,
in amber light feasting in golden-washed prime
The time it kept drifting, with reading and play
And sampling the stew for his homecoming tray.
And she picked him a flower for the table, smelled its bloom
The lamplight is flickering o'er the warm brown-washed room.

His light weaved the canyon, split the darkness to her gate.
as her heart came up into her, so ecstatic, soul elate,
joyous, open, loving, grasping, melts within them, to vibrate
there together, wrapped in pleasure at the gate.
Breathless, heart pounding embrace.

Later by the fire, they laughed and shared
reminding one another that they cared.
Looking in their eyes to synthesize
in sharing guise the giving prize
with hearts that rise, passion that flies
they are suddenly their eyes.
And they helplessly give in.
He kissed her once
and then again
for it had been all day
He had missed her
and missed her again,
and he kissed her
once again.

LIVING MOMENTS
(cont.)

And now together with lamp in tow
and her sweet, soft hand to promised land they go.
Where softness reigns in pillowed scent
in billowing groans of released content
and softly settling in quiet, sleepy stint.

The lamp finally flickers and dries away
In the darkness left behind slips the end of day
but in the seamless plan that makes it right
the moon shines oe'r the sky, carries on the bright.
And the moonglow settles upon their flesh tonight
love in action, joyful traction
here at this site.

Now they lie in sleep awaiting the next big say,
when the light comes bursting down upon this place
and we happy souls who embrace it renew the race,
as we learn and feel some more where we're given space,
to bring it peace and kind and gentle love embrace
And this is true at every moment of every day.
That if we live in that very moment it has its say
Living moments are the blessings of the day.

Spiritual Empowerment 19:

SPIRIT LEADS; HUMANS FOLLOW

Be led by the spirit inside.

Human ministers, preachers, pastors, apostles, gurus, teachers, revivalists, consultants, fortune tellers, tarot card readers, astrologists, evangelists, guides, interpreters, translators, channels, transmitters, mystics, seers, prophets, poets, educators, professors and scripturists should in no case be considered to be your ... leaders. They should all, in fact, be led by the Holy Spirit themselves.

Through history, as people we call leaders have put themselves above God, terrible things have happened. This should be instructive.

Rayson, a Teaching Mission teacher once said: "For a human to go to another human for spiritual guidance is ... baffling."

My best advice: Explore in love, not fear. Get perspectives. Consult your inner guidance based upon all you can learn. The more you explore, the more you learn, the more you can TRUST your inner guidance.

Inner guidance does not work as well when you are totally ignorant about a subject. Go as far as you can and ask for help to understand more.

Develop your mind, your body, your senses, your spirit, your powers of discernment, your powers of love, your power to forgive, your energy to give service. Whew! You won't have time for gurus. Go to the Source. Go directly to God in prayer. Go in Love and let the spirit lead.

And consider what preachers say as ... "suggestions based on their understandings." Don't insult the Spirit of Truth by not using it.

Spiritual Empowerment 20:

WE ARE THE ONES WE HAVE BEEN WAITING FOR.

Have you been waiting for a great savior, a guru, a teacher, a method, a revelatory vision in the sky? Have you expected a melchizedek to materialize, Jesus to return, the Virgin Mary to appear in the sky? Well ... considering that Faith is the greatest tenant of Christianity .... considering that being agondonters, who can believe without seeing, is the noble status of Urantians

... considering it is a co-creative time and space universe in which the mortals alone have the physical presence to promote truth, beauty and goodness ...

... and considering that this is our quest, our reason for being ...

Do you really expect all this to be destroyed? Would this be God's plan? His plan is evolution.

To cry out for rescue from our follies is not going to work either.

We must clean up the environment with divine inspiration and instruction.

We must abolish war and arms races and international arms trade.

We must choose higher values to build a higher society.

We must rebuild our institutions with a spiritual dimension.

We are the ones who must become leaders for change. We are empowered. We are the Children of the Most Highs.

We are here, now, and it's time to be about the Father's business.

Spiritual Empowerment 21:

DON'T FEAR, THEY ARE EVER HERE: DISCOVERY, REVELATION, AND CHANGE

Discoveries and revelations bring change. And this is the way of our lives. The way of evolving time and space worlds. Let's take the broad view, the cosmic view. Remember: millions of planets, trillions of beings.

There is nothing to fear here. Some people make themselves unhappy by resisting change, with suspicion of new discoveries, with disdain for any new spiritual revelation at all.

They imagine a static universe ... with a static mind. Or the good old days - which weren't. They disdain the human race because we are so far from perfect.

Urantia Book readers may consider this text as the fifth and last revelation. If it isn't in the book, it isn't. But ... really, how much has the world changed since the 1920s or 30s or 1955 when it was published?

Why do we anchor ourselves in old and imperfect perceptions .... in the Bible, in some idea of Paul's or a Fifth Epochal Revelation which, after all, was prohibited from giving humankind any unearned knowledge? So it didn't. Let's go out and earn some knowledge in honest exploration.

Anchors drag in mud. Let the wind move your sails and sail on! There are islands to discover. New information, new ideas, new perspectives, new visions are all food for the mind. They don't hurt and they're nothing to be afraid of.

If you are not receptive to new ideas, then you won't have any. If you go through life afraid of things you don't know, you will never know about them.

If you are afraid of being duped, you don't trust your own mind. And that's the first problem you need to overcome.

You do that by knowing your mind, spiritualizing it for strength, and feeding it with the nectar of human life.

Let's hear the way Van says it.

(Music: The Mystery)

So finally, today, we are still faced with the Great Mystery ... of life. It can bring to us many experiences, good and bad. We strive to understand it and make it work for us, as we build our Souls. On behalf of the OneTeam, the Celestial Artisans, and my mortal self, thank you for coming.

The artisans would leave you with this thought.

In its silence, in its succulence
`in its sparkling, streaming crease
Make it yours in all its glories, this pure
Power of the Peace.

You can trust it in the ringing
of your silent bells of release
that turns uneasy into believing
in the Power of the Peace

Make its silence be a roar within
your joyful blessed relief
Walk hand in hand with God each day
Feel Power in the Peace.

Go in Peace.

by Jim Cleveland

SEPARATING GOD FROM RELIGIONS

A workshop on achieving a personal religion with a simple God

Presented at the Association for Light and Life spiritual unity conference in Boise, Idaho, 2004.

Good Day, Brothers and Sisters, what a wonderful gathering this has been.

Thank you for coming. From your presence, I assume you can perceive that God and our planetary religions could be considered ... distinct and separate ... and that somehow we can separate and exalt the great simplicity that is God from the complexity of dogmas that seek to indoctrinate us at every turn. This is something I've struggled with personally – an unnecessary bitterness toward organized religion ... grasping the true meaning of spirituality ... learning why we can't live in peace and good will.

It is a good time to resolve these issues, since we are arguably in the middle of an ultimate battle between good and evil. Some call it Armageddon. The End times. A New Age. To the Teaching Mission, it's the Correcting Time. Some Urantia Book fundamentalists aren't looking for anything much, for another few thousand years anyway.

By the way, remember the Age of Aquarius we used to herald. It is actually just getting underway, for those who wondered whatever happened to it. We made it a cliché and then quit mentioning it.

These are certainly quickening and pivotal times. Whether you feel pessimistic about it, or optimistic about it. Or sometimes both.

Today, we see advocates of several major religious orders in the world unleashing savage violence to destroy their enemies. Their ... imagined enemies. President Bush poses as a religiously righteous man. So does Osama bin Laden. The Palestinian homicide bombers are righteous. The Israelis in the tanks are righteous. The Taliban is righteous too.

Well, are they all simply self-righteous? Are any of them spiritual people at all? Are they just examples of how mankind is always putting itself above God, consciously and mostly unconsciously? Always, too many people have done violent and evil deeds and then said God okayed it or actually helped them do it. Always, people have produced books and deemed them holy. Always, they have had self-serving ideas and called them ... inspired.

We don't need these people to anchor our religion.

It is time, dear brothers and sisters, to sweep away all of these horrors cloaked in the name of various religions. But to win Armageddon and to bring forth a spiritual awakening on this planet is going to require some clear thinking. We can see that our world of proliferating dogmas haven't provided it.

103

Truly, the really spiritual people today, in 2004, are able to finally take all of this myriad of religious doctrine ... with a grain of salt. Move above and beyond it.

Let's do that now, by beginning this session with a Stillness exercise ... And a prayer. May we take a few moments to relax, take some deep breaths, still your mind, and enjoy the silence. (pause) Deep breathes, lowering yourself from beta into a relaxing but energized alpha state. Relax your mind. There is no dogma on the planet, no history. The books all disappeared. We are left to contemplate only the earth and sky.

Open your inner vision now to a vast star field, a panorama before you ... Each star glistening with a new sparkle of illuminating, instructive and inspiring information for you. You and God are the only immediate reality.

Relax into this beautiful deep skyline. Be at peace in the Stillness.

May we now ask of Father what we believe that we need.

Here is a prayer that I personally make ... and to which you may also ascribe.

Dear Universal Father, you represent to me TRUTH. Please free us from the tangle of perspectives that complicate the simple reality of YOU.

My new religion as of today is to always appreciate and seek higher understandings of TRUTH ... and to create higher levels of Truth in Your name. Do not stagnate in what we think is truth. Do not build fences around it.

Inhale deeply and ... release ... breathe freely ...

Dear Infinite Mother Spirit, you represent to me BEAUTY. Your energies have nurtured our lives and our world. Mankind has often sullied the beauty of our creation by polluting the soil, the water, the air, and the landscapes. Please free us from the ugliness we have spewed out upon you. Show us how to be celestial gardeners. Give us visions of the Beauty that we can create ... and Be.

My new religion today, Mother Spirit, is to always appreciate and seek higher understandings of BEAUTY ... and to create higher levels of Beauty in Your name.

Relax and inhale deeply ... Release ... breathe freely ...

Dear Michael, you represent to me GOODNESS. When you incarnated as Jesus, you showed us a greater reality of God and of ourselves. The virtues of altruism, mercy, compassion, kindness, forgiveness, love, courage, faith, selflessness. The myth of brute power. The reality of triumph over mortal death, the power of resurrection ... Showing us the way to live and die in faith and peace ... and how perfectly safe death is ... a threshold.

My new religion today is to always appreciate and seek higher understandings of GOOD-NESS, and to actually create higher levels of Goodness in Jesus' name.

So may I simply embrace a religion of Truth and Beauty and Goodness today.

May all else waft away for these moments right now with the Holy Trinity. Imagine there are no books, no CNN or Fox, no churches or temples at all. Just the glorious beauty of the Creation in water, plants, animals, rock and earth. I am naked and clean and washed with rain in the Garden. I have tools for cultivation.

As I start fresh today, may I not be self-centered, self-serving, self-absorbed. Please. This is part of the animal origin nature from which I am gloriously ascending. Thank you for these wonderfully evolved mammalian bodies. Thank you for imbuing me with a sharing of the Cosmic Mind. Thank you for the Holy Triad of Spirits, which indwell me and assist me in finding ...

Truth
Beauty
Goodness

In Mind and Body and Spirit.

It will be my Personal Religion to understand these things and to actually create them!

Create higher layers of truth.
Create new faces of beauty
Create an aura and environment of goodness wherever I go.

My prayer is that this will bring PEACE.

May we awaken now with greater clarity and purity. *(pause)*

And so, let's use our minds a bit and explore again the idea of separating God from religions ..... Religions, plural of course. The ones who have always been out there battling one another for your allegiance. Not the personal religion we just recommended to you.

Now that we have clearly focused our religion and freed our mind from the minds of others.... We don't have to accept any of the churches except for the services they can provide and the venues they provide for our service.

So organized religious advocacies are no longer a source of Absolute Truth for us now. Like everything else on Urantia, there are two sides to this goodness and badness thing. We can put all this conflict aside except for philosophical discussion.

We now have a personal relationship with God that allows us to ask direct questions and to get answers in the Stillness. The Stillness time with God that anchors the Urantia Book and has been the constant Teaching Mission lesson for more than a decade.

Your prayers WILL be answered. Perhaps as an inner knowingness a day or two later... perhaps from the next person you meet. Your prayers will be answered; count on it. The challenge is to be aware of the answers when they come. And the answers often come with a brother or sister and, chances are, they will need your reciprocal service as well. This happens very, very often. We are being guided in how to work together. This is the central quest for people and societies on Urantia.

So you don't need someone to communicate with God for you, to pray for you, to save you with the tithe that you give them. You don't need to be degreed or ordained. God will love and guide each of us. Our indwelling Spirit of God guides us; the Holy Mother Spirit nurtures us; Jesus inspires to be all that we can ever be. And he has spoken to us forcefully that he is determined not to lose a single soul, a single sheep of his flock.

So, if you came into this session saying to yourself: "Why should we separate God from our religions; shouldn't we embrace all religions and strive to see the commonalities and work together from this foundation. Be altruistic and love everyone in all churches and faiths and urge them to love everyone as well."

My reply ... Sure, that's true, but ...

I wouldn't suggest embracing any of the mountain of dogma that religions have published. It's all polluted by self-serving partisans. The best religion is a personal relationship with God. More than ever in the Correcting Time, the successful churches will be the ones that profess this and promote it. As the Urantia Book says, the religion of Jesus will ultimately triumph.

When Jesus wanted to talk to the Universal Father, where did he go? He separated himself from all of humanity and went .... Into the wilderness. The so-called wilderness. One man's wilderness is another man's cathedral.

You can, of course, enjoy a church family as much as ever. As long as you represent the simple religion of Truth, Beauty and Goodness, you will fit into any church and any situation. At their heart and in their roots, all of the world's faiths believe in the truth-beauty-goodness paradigm as well. They are ultimately on your side, and they will recognize it when you stand up for these spiritual ideals. There are countless millions of people who rejoice in a church family without worrying about doctrine. They have their cake and eat it too. Some Catholics ignore birth control and think celibacy is dumb. Some Baptists have a drink behind closed doors and don't tithe. Some religionists don't believe they are the one and only true faith.

Since you don't worship the church itself, or its narratives, and don't consider the minister infallible, you can always speak up when you believe a policy of the church does not represent Truth, Beauty and Goodness for all people – not just members of the church. You can be altruistic and loving, and you can promote altruism and love; your minister and your fellow church members may even challenge you to do so with their … separatist attitudes. If you have a strong personal religion, you can serve your church.

In this way, learning and growing people will be constantly changing churches and other institutions in the years ahead, as we all move through a Correcting Time that is more far-reaching than most of us can imagine. It includes all of the worlds of the Lucifer Rebellion, and all worlds beyond those throughout the local universe of Nebadon, and other universes that presumably follow the activities here through universal broadcasts.

Michael's local universe is indeed in the spotlight in these tumultuous times. And we are at the center of the spotlight, the world of the cross, the world where our Creator Son himself personally established a religious legacy in his own human name. I am certain that we can count on a full purification of that religion in time – and we can all be part of that mission. Did you ever think you would have that opportunity?

As you keep your relationship with God exclusively yours, you will also receive incremental and exclusive gifts that will continually brighten your life. Day by day. Week by week.

Higher perceptions of universal truth … As your vessel can hold them.
Higher perceptions of beauty
Higher perceptions of goodness

Much of the shallow, self-serving, dogma-laden ideas of the past will fall away. You will see and experience many new enlightened perceptions of what is real and what is faulty logic. Some of your new ideas may surprise you. They will stretch you and inspire you into a Cosmic View, a philosophical and spiritual understanding of each challenge, each opportunity, every situation.

You will make some startling discoveries when you free your mind of complications; you will be making room for them when you effect a purer perception of reality. An open mind is a wonderful thing; it can learn and grow. A closed mind will always suffer and doubt; it is in a self- imposed prison, after all.

In your personalized religion, you will begin to see the reality of true beauty – in the faces of the human comedy drama that plays out before you every day. In the amazing beauty of the natural creation. The majesty of trees. The uniquely beautiful life forms of the fish, animal and insect kingdoms. The amazing story of how a tiny nurtured seed expands into a splendidly detailed plant. There is beauty in Art … Architecture … Automobiles … Angelic visions … Artichokes … Armadillos … and in the Eyes of every human being that I have ever been able to penetrate.

Through all of this, you will begin to understand what Goodness truly is.

It will surprise you. You will find that goodness, like God, like truth, like beauty, is simple too, so that every human child of God can know it, and understand it without either books or dogma.

All of these newfound treasures of the spirit will drive you to more contemplation, more yearning, expressing, sharing, giving ... And all of these things are good for you in this world, your ... school of material experience, in flesh and blood. A living laboratory.

If your personal religion here is Truth and Beauty and Goodness, you will seek these things... and you will therefore find them wherever you go. And you will have the opportunity to share them ... in service.

And you will find this all so wonderfully energizing that you will want to share more. And as you receive the new energies and the blessings from each light that you shine, you are empowered to give more and to receive more and shine ever more brightly. Every step of faith is rewarded with empowerments.

Your attitude will grow even more loving and caring and peaceful so that, finally and forever, that ancient curse to humankind with which we have been inflicted for all the ages will be quelled.

That curse is ...Restlessness. Are we not all restless souls?

What makes us restless? Knowing fear, not peace; knowing competition not cooperation, knowing danger not security, knowing alienation not family. It's all enough to make us restless.

When our quest is focused on more Truth, Beauty and Goodness in our lives, rising above the fallible philosophies of unknowing humans, then our lives can be far less complicated and centered upon the great simplicity that is God.

This great simplicity means that even the children of God in an isolated village in the jungles of the deepest nowhere have the spirit within that can bring their souls to righteousness. There are indeed people in the world who have nothing but a mud or stick hut and beds of straw to sleep on, and they struggle each day simply for sustenance and survival. No education. No philosophy. No theology.

And yet even these people have our simple religion within them too.

They appreciate and seek truth. They appreciate and seek beauty. They appreciate and seek goodness. I have not met these people except in National Geographic ... but I am utterly convinced that they do.

Separating God from Religions means separating God's essential features from all this dog-ma that has spawned wars and massive horrors over the centuries, from churches and faiths which have never grasped the essential truth that they should be worshipping all together, forgive one another past horrors, make a new beginning in appreciation of altruistic love that rises above their infantile beliefs.

And amazingly, when you fully embrace this clear-eyed view of your relationship with God, you begin to see that there are no enemies.

It's unwise to be bitter about and battle organized religions, for example. Make them better if you are involved. Love your brothers and sisters who are struggling within them for those very same things – truth, beauty and goodness.

When people of all religions have a personal relationship with God and aren't taking their directions from some ancient prophet or some present-day charismatic, they will make these religious institutions into what they really should be. And many preachers and priests will step down from their pedestals and join the Correcting Time. It will happen. It is already happening. And you can help directly. Or you can serve in a myriad of other fields of inter-est. You can spread love and wisdom anywhere, at any time, in any place.

And all the while, your own personal religion is safely tucked into your heart, your mind, your spirit. It's all inside you. Going with you across fields of darkness and light. Growing your Soul. Forever more.

May we all ascend in Grace.

VISIONS OF GETTING ALONG

Visions.   Some are smoke and some are air
            and they are wafting everywhere.
            Some are selfish, some are giving
            Some are brave and some are cringing
            in the face of what could finally be despair.

Visions.   Some are hopeful, they speak of beauty
            Some are fearful, stink of malaise
            We can dream of raking in the booty
            We could drown in purple haze

Visions.   Some are sure that the future will bring
            all that will make us each into wholeness
            ride out of our prisons on rainbow prisms
            break into a sky bright with soulfulness

Visions.   Some can already see it now, it's the One
            The center where we can all sweetly come
            When we make our visions bright
            Sustain the nurturing light
            That made possible all the paths that we have run.
            And offers barefoot love 'til the setting sun

            We all have visions from material eyes
            They paint the future with opaque.
            We have our minds, we fight for causes
            Hoping it's not all a mistake.
            We each have destinies we would like to see
            We have loved ones we hope to lean on.
            We'll pull our own weight, do our best to equate
            What it takes and how everyone could get along.

by Jim Cleveland

QUICKENING

The world is a place of suffering
A lack of love has had its due
Even as the joys of the Creation
shine each day in front of you.
Now you feel foundations shaking,
Naked light on fiefdoms quaking
from the truths that shake the faiths
that misguided you.
In these times we need your actions
for the love to gain some traction
that will light the way of purpose
for each of you.

There was a time we needed anchors
Today, we must unfurl our sails.
There was a time we needed to slow the rudder
Now we can ride the joyful gales.
There was a time we needed patience
Today we need to chart the quest
to bring love in every minute
unite these islands of loneliness.

There was a time we needed Oneness
Now it's time to make it BE
There's no reason to be waiting
for someone else to ride these seas.
The waves are yours for making.
Build them high and swift and breaking
all across the sky so blue, so quiet, at ease
with the reality of a love ark for all who please.

SINS OF SLAVERY AND SEPARATION

It was Judas Iscariot who identified for me the greatest sin of all – the worst affront to God. It wasn't his.

While he admitted his own follies, wrought from his isolated personality, he channeled back to the planet earth that humankind's continued, adamant, purposeful separation from God, the Father, is the worst sin of all. God indwells our personality with his spirit. We know it and can feel it, but some live in rejection of the presence, that strong inclination to love and goodness, in order to act out the bellicose territorialism of our animal natures and even turn them to malice and evil purposes.

One can 'be still and know that I am God.' One can recognize and follow the guidance of God's presence within. Suppose it was your real-life father, he lived across the street, and you never visited? That deliberate separation from even the effort to know God as a creator and source of life seemed like the worst thing one could do in life.

This was mostly abstract. I had to return to my native Mississippi to more fully understand the causes and consequences of serious sin and feel it once more in my gut. I had made a long journey of open-minded spiritual discovery since leaving that homeland of hypocritical hubris.

I considered this an excellent analysis. It is part of a collection of narratives to a Rev. James Padgett in the 1920's. The gentleman questioned the authenticity of scripture and a series of his channeled messages from Jesus and others confirmed that the text was indeed riddled with error of perception. While living in the Midwest, I came into contact with a number of spiritual books that guided me into objective spiritual analysis.

The Urantia Book explains the cosmology of the universe and our place in it, as ascending personalities living a material experience, where we live an evolution in which we must make good moral choices to survive and continue. This evolutionary plan for mortals was created by God, known on most worlds by the genderless "First Source and Center."

A Course in Miracles deconstructs materialistic thinking that we may realize spiritual reality as being greater than the material, even making it irrelevant in the greatest sense. We are spirits with bodies, not vice versa. We are experiencing materiality and the finiteness of the mortal life.

The Pathwork Foundation lectures provide a third worthy spiritual revelation by the fruits therein, beautiful and insightful lessons on how to clarify issues and work together on this planet for fruitful balance and service.

I learned more about Oneness in Humanity's Team and more about caring community from the Unity Fellowship. I read channellings from the Lightworkers, who want to live above and beyond the falseness that inflicts the world's scriptures. I joined a band of mostly Wiccan naturalists who revere and honor the beautiful land we collectively own, and the sacredness of earth.

In the Midwest, I felt a greater optimism among people, a can-do, business-like attitude. But then, with Mom's health failing, I returned to my hometown of Calhoun City, where I was born in a tiny room in a small house in 1938. I had lived there through years of racial conflicts, sordid and regrettable. I now believed that, in its heart, racism was a spiritual issue.

As a reporter for the Jackson Daily News in 1960-61, my paper was branded a racist rag. Editor Jimmy Ward railed against northern agitators and "fuzzy-headed liberals" and I watched Freedom Riders hustled off to Parchman state prison. I smelled the stench of three black body bags from Neshoba County being hauled into the University Hospital. I watched police dogs literally rip off the dress of a young black woman attempting to use the Jackson City Library. Yokels and policemen grinned and giggled.

When I became news editor for Mississippi State's public relations department, I watched students burn an effigy of James Meredith by the statue of a Confederate general, and head off in a caravan to Oxford where segregationist militia were assembling to thwart the integration of Ole Miss. Within hours my 155th Infantry Division of the Mississippi National Guard was federalized by President John Kennedy to take us from the possible control of Gov. Ross Barnett and his white Citizens Council gang.

Our trucks plowed through brickbats, rebel yells, obscenities and the residual acrid mist of tear gas. We were all young Southern men of mixed and confused persuasions. We had fixed bayonets and not a single bullet in our M-1 chambers. We had been drafted into an enforcer role against most of our neighbors. It's just as well they stashed us in the Holly Springs National Forest for a week until it all blew over.

By the time I left Mississippi, I was over 40 and would live in the Midwest for over sixteen years. I didn't appreciate the Southern Baptists of my upbringing for their hypocrisy and racism. I remember the Baptist Sunday School ditty: "Red and yellow, black and white, they are precious in his sight. Jesus loves the little children of the world." I also remember the deacons of the First Baptist Church in Jackson meeting a black family at the door for services, and turning them away.

Earlier era churches supported the slaveholding planters who financed them. Latter day Southern Baptists enforced segregation, at least until plummeting membership and other political situations compelled the recent embrace of a new policy and a genuine black president. Homosexuals, however, are still branded as abominations, and will likely remain so until the religion faces more political realities of the modern world.

From the Baptist ranks of baptism at age nine, I married a Catholic woman. I listened to a dour priest explain their tenants of absolute truth while chain smoking unfiltered cigarettes, lighting one off the other. Please, God, I said, don't let him light another one. He lit it anyway, and continued to explain the Virgin Birth.

I couldn't forgive the Catholics for their bloodthirsty history of oppressions, against indigenous people, against Pagans, Protestants. Some truly evil Popes had armies of their own. I could respect them more if they had ever asked for forgiveness, supposedly one of their axioms. They have never admitted any wrongdoing or guilt, never asked for forgiveness and still carry on pontiff-driven commands to procreate diligently, even in places where millions have perished from war, starvation and unsustainable families. The pedophile scandals were additional nails for my condemnation.

I left the Evangelicals and Catholics believing that the real truth about Jesus' mission was either largely misunderstood, or else his true values of all-one-people under a loving a compassionate Father God had been hijacked into an arena for human control. Don't think, just 'trust and obey,' said a Baptist hymn. Forget your mind and the God-given free will right to use it. Follow orders, don't drink beer, don't seek intimate encounters with that evil sex urge of yours. It was like behavior management, as silly in its way as the Catholic's bizarre and unworkable celibacy idea.

In 2005, I returned to the northeast Mississippi flatwoods to an environment of malaise, much still like the 1950s, except there were many more vacant buildings. The garment plant got corporatized, then moved to the Philipines. Weed, crack and Oxycontin had appeared and were spiking the crime rate among the poorer people out on the gravel roads. There were now cellphones, good for drug deals. Local merchants have given way to Sonic and Subway and two dollar store chains fighting it out. Plate lunches and fried foods are served out of gas stations. This sanctimonious county has always disdained legal alcohol even as most Mississippi counties are wet. Beer still requires a trip to the county line stores.

Did time stand still here? Did it stagnate? Is it stupefied at the way the people have never worked together in our sordid history.

Our pioneer ancestors fought and killed the Choctaw and Chickasaw Indians. In 1831, Andrew Jackson's federal government began forcibly evicting them in death marches to Oklahoma, taking possession of eleven million acres. Those Indians who remained were subjected to generations of harassment and brutalization until President Franklin Roosevelt's administration gave them a tribal identity and some land where they would be safe from the white savages and have some economic opportunity.

Given that cotton was the most prized commodity on the planet, the foundation of clothes, other ancestors attacked tribes in Africa, killed, pillaged and brought black slaves here. From slave markets in the East, this ragged multitude of humans were flooded down into the Cotton Belt ... the Slave Belt ... the Bible Belt. From South Carolina across Texas, their population soared, people in constant degradation , suffering in chains under whip and gun.

They could be killed if necessary to maintain their grievous servitude, and it would be only a property matter. It all became a culture.

It required the most ruinous war in our history to end the great sin of slavery. It then required years of battle to overturn generations of intimidating white courthouse gangs, white-sheeted terrorists, and the bane of segregation as a stacked deck for the white ruling class. Whites were still angry about the war, at GOP carpetbag corruption, lawless blacks and stooges thrust into public office.

Lynchings weren't uncommon in the South, and the perpetrators were never punished. In time, the national Democratic Party became the champions of civil rights. At the national convention, a band of so-called Mississippi Freedom Democrats, mostly blacks, were officially seated instead of the usual white Magnolia State delegation. It signaled a seismic political shift.

President Lyndon Johnson acknowledged that his party's support of black equality would lose the South for years to come. It has indeed done that. Even today, Mississippians are prepared to hold their nose and vote for Republican nominee Mitt Romney this fall, even against their best interests. Their more desired candidates fell in the primaries and they are stuck with their only choice – a big business scion in bed with the banks and corporations and the powers that have turned most of the wealth of the country into the hands of a tiny portion of the population . But he is preferable to President Obama who remains black, as does the state's Democrat power base.

Throughout the cotton belt, the black belt, the bible belt, the old and unrepentant Confederacy, the white backlash to government-mandated legal equality will continue to deliver, even to this lukewarm Republican candidate. A pawn shop dealer in Grenada told me: "It ain't 'cause he's black. It's 'cause he ain't got no economic sense."

The familiar Democratic players are still occupying the courthouses today for the most part, though some have formally switched parties, making it necessary for white backlashers in Mississippi to vote for friends in the local elections and then switch to support Republicans at the national level.

I wondered what a vastly different country this would be if we had snapped that umbilical cord of slavery before it got started. Of course, since the Constitution was fine with it, perhaps many Americans could swallow it too, accept the idea that equality is for civilized humans, and not subhuman savages who were so startlingly different in appearance. And like the Negroes, one does not want to forget that women had no voting rights at the time either. The imperfect Constitution has needed a plethora of amendments.

Now, into the 21st century, we have reaped many bitter whirlwinds because our forefathers chose to sustain slavery for the cotton, and allow the South to grow into world agricultural prominence upon the backs of suffering slaves.

Surely, slavery was the worse sin of all, for it had reverberated in so many ways into so many horrible and hateful conflicts over the years. Sin is not some abstract thing, not an ideology, but real flesh and blood evil.

Today, the racial divide across this state and region is still a deleterious reality. With roughly half of Mississippi's population largely divided against itself and a resulting poverty of quality education, wealth and spirit, what business or industry would come here over the years? The cheap labor that once brought some industries into the South was later found to be even cheaper abroad, and in countries with little or no worker rights.

While the white backlash voter bloc, propelled by a GOP Southern Strategy to focus on peripheral evangelical issues, drove white business, banking and evangelicals into the party, that still hasn't prevented it from serving the needs of the rich, trying to castrate government safeguards for working people, social security and medical care programs. Ironically, government programs which help the poor are the largest source of income in Mississippi, yet one of the GOP's biggest targets for elimination or privatization takeover.

The white voting majority largely resents such programs, considers themselves to be a higher class of people than the blacks and poor whites on welfare, do not think races should mix and do not want to pay any taxes beyond the barest of necessity. They see a great threat posed to America by the 'welfare state' and something they vacuously call 'socialism' and they want to stop it cold. In a biblical sense, it is the house divided that can't stand. It only stands as the poorest state in the union by most measurements.

Clearly, returning to Mississippi with some worldly experience hadn't softened my attitude about the region's myopic and often venal perceptions. I could now see the desolation of souls here with a keener eye, a deeper perceptive. And when I took my own advice to go into a daily Stillness time to be quiet, pray, worship, contemplate and listen, there came to me some additional bridges of perception.

Judas was correct. Men and women who perpetuate the evils of slavery have indeed chosen a deliberate separation from God's will in the first place. Each soul knows God's will. And when they come to see slaves as people, replete with tears and laughter, feeling joy and pain, loving their children, goodness in their hearts, suffering in humiliation, being treated like property, one knows that they are a child of God, equal in God's eyes, and so can only lie to themselves about it.

One has to significantly separate himself from God to participate in this evil. Our choice, as the infantile child that we are, to disdain the Golden Rule, the strong urge to goodness rising out of our soul, to blind ourselves to the reality which God has made so apparent here, is surely a sin of real consequences.

But then I was reminded by subtle and quiet spiritual voices that Jesus made a point of forgiving those workers who nailed him to the cross. As lowly laborers or slaves, they had helped crucify others in Rome's brutal assembly line of death. And so if you are ignorant of sin, error, evil, how can you commit it? Did Judas' confusions represent evil or error? Was his sorrow, repentance and suicide a rectification, making him more open for forgiveness? Since Jesus' incarnation life emphasized empathy, compassion, mercy and forgiveness among all people, can this hallmark be maintained? Judas maintains that he has been forgiven and is now in service.

One's intentions are vitally important. This is the cornerstone by which our mortal lives will be judged. We are not always strong enough to fulfill our good intentions, perhaps rarely, but this is a yardstick for measuring one's worth, and whether a person will have value to continue in God's ascension plan.

In Mississippi, there is only the Judeo-Christian fused bible. These ideas from other books may as well be on another planet in my forlorn homeland. The scam has worked wonderfully here. The churches largely have crafted religions which are less focused on God's indwelling spirit and more into so-called holy books, purportedly written or every word inspired by God himself. Many protestants truly worship 'The Word.' And from the errant teachings of the apostle Paul, they perceive a guilt-ridden theory that Jesus was sent here to die for humanity's sins.

The truth is, that he came here to show us how to live in God. His death was just the final human step in a profound mission of empathy for the mortal sojourners of his creation – choosing that he, too, would live, suffer and die just as we will in this mortal ascension plan. And it won't matter. The transition is safe. The body can be killed, not the spirit, which belongs to God.

It's not that his resurrection was miraculous. It is actually the passageway that he shows us for our personal journey if we only accept in faith our relationship with a kind and caring fatherly God. Jesus brought an entirely new benevolent vision of God, often seen as tyrannical, even jealous and angry, during the time of his incarnation, and even today.

So if God, and son Jesus, understand and empathize with the struggles of humankind, then surely allowances are made for ignorance. But if one were a slaveholder or merchant, there is a powerful intention to evil. And if you are a pastor who portends to represent God, or Jesus, and proceeds to be deceitful in his name, that goes beyond ignorance as well. It's one thing to disdain God's presence and guidance; it's worse to pretend you truly represent those highest of values when you don't.

Ignorance is not intentional evil but can easily lead there. The truth of our intentions is known. We will stand up at some time and represent the life we lead here.

Should we live our lives largely in deprivation and ignorance, our minds still harbor intentions and our bodies act upon what our minds decide. If you're subjected to labor driving nails into the hands and feet of people being crucified, you will weigh the survival of your enforced servitude to what you would intentionally do. One doesn't want to die from a Roman sword and fail thereby to live and support one's wife and child.

Should our lives be in environments that foster education and culture, I believe that more is expected of these spiritual sojourners – to utilize those talents in service to one's fellows, to form communities for harmony and healing. To those who receive more blessings, more is expected in sharing and service.

From my readings, I have concluded that all true religion is personal – between us and spirit. A channeled celestial teacher, Rayson, has noted that for one human to go to another human for spiritual guidance was ... "baffling." Indeed, when one can connect to spiritual guidance in times of silence and intentional release, intentional faith, intentional love and worship for the First Source, and when insights, clarities and answers can flow to you, then churches, shackled in manmade, self-serving dogma, have little vitality to you any more.

The world is undergoing a spiritual renaissance into this higher, deeper and more personal spirituality, fused together by instant communications, challenged by collapsing institutions, which have to be rebuilt with a sustainable level of spiritual values. Polarity is showing clearly the true champions and enemies of a benevolent, caring society for the first time ever and in the broadest global context. Profound challenges loom, and our intentions are everything. Our fates are in the balance.

It doesn't seem so in these quiet Mississippi hills. The people across this rural countryside of the new Confederacy have little knowledge or interest in spiritual questions. There will be a blanket of red votes, tea party stained, all across the region where race trumps everything else, and knowledge of national and global issues is often subjugated to the simplistic Republican strategy of focusing and framing Democrats as being too submissive to blacks, immigrants, gays, welfare recipients, workers unions, women seeking abortions, trial lawyers, and more recently Muslims.

On the other side, the Republicans become dismissive of these people blocs in confidence that the country's Capitalist power structure, all about class and money, can outvote these people and even discredit them.

So with this additional viewpoint, I now considered an even deeper layer of sin. There are those who prey upon sincere Christians and trick them into voting against both their economic and spiritual interests. Under their inept placeholder, George W. Bush, they looted the country, absconded with the money into foreign havens, and left President Obama with a broken nation. How bad is it to pretend an allegiance to Christianity to get votes while your political party forsakes its true principles and acts more like the money-changers and sacrificial goat sellers who got routed from the temple by Jesus.

My contempt for the self-serving rich and aspiring rich has irritated me in recent months. It bothers me that these people corrupt all of our institutions, especially those vulnerable, narrowly educated politicians we elect to office, some of them who actually want to be honorable. It is truly a sin to intentionally corrupt people who want to be honest, and corrupt our institutions with lavish bribes and influence-peddling, especially if it's cloaked in a hypocritical spirituality.

But can sin prevail? Isn't the world waking up to a higher consciousness, as all my new-thought spiritual connections say? When I got beyond my self-imposed irritability about evil, I relaxed into stillness, and there came a breath of relief. As the GOP is now divided between its traditional chamber of commerce base and the manipulations of Tea Party string-pullers to gut the government and the labor unions, there is now a chasm that can't be traversed. The ruins that W. created and that spawned the noisy tea radicals has resulted in a candidate that few people like and a divided Congress that most people hate. Big money can pour out millions but they can't win. It will be a lesson.

The GOP developed a Southern strategy and won with it for awhile, the white backlash. Now in 2012 , they're ironically stuck with it, anchored in the votes they will get in the new Confederate States of America, similar to Barry Goldwater, and destined to go down in defeat in most of mainstream America. Populists and Republicans don't belong together and Romney's mixed message of meaningless mush shows it.

We should all pay rapt attention to the amazing times we live in, the roots and core of the spiritual and societal issues being thrust before us. It is a critical time for choosing values and intentions, for each person and for each society that person lives in. Times are quickening; nations are quivering on the brink of massive social changes, admixed with environmental turmoil resulting from our poor stewardship of the planet.

Eventually, I grew tired of analyzing layers of error and evil. I left Judas to his rehabilitation and education program. Pay these things less attention and don't dwell on them. Positive thoughts and intentions release positive energies. Connect with Spirit and state the intention of bringing more truth, beauty and goodness into the world, and into your own life, into your behavior. Ask for guidance and listen for the small and subtle voice inside you.

Ask for the Father and he will assert that he is that small voice that lives within you. Knock on Jesus' door and he has promised to answer, no matter you be Christian or Jew or Muslim or Spiritist. We are all children of the one God. We are siblings and we have spiritual parents. Our common and noble quest is to find Oneness in God's family of man.

We would do well to speculate less on the nature of the greatest sin and devote more time to finding the greatest possible virtue that we can achieve.

Radical Spirituality
Conversation with Mantoube Melchizedek

Some of us on the planet converse with supernal personalities, teachers from the spiritual realms. We are considered radical, without valid doctrine or dogma, and only represented as invisible conversations, keystroked and reproduced on the internet. Most citizens of the world would ask seriously the value of this spiritual advice.

There are many mosques, temples and churches on the planet and we "channelers" are not well represented in any of them. They give lip service to having a personal relationship with God in these chambers, but it never seems to come to pass.

By "channeling" or "transmitting" spiritual beings we place ourselves into the fringes of reliability for the mainstream religions, where prayer is an essential, but direct conversant messages of advice and counsel are not the rule. We can pray directly, but neither God nor a representative, is expected to speak in turn. This kind of reply might well cause some consternation at a Southern Baptist Wednesday night prayer meeting.

Who are we channelers, after all, to interdict the self-organized religions and develop a personal relationship with God? What are our rights to directly-imparted spiritual knowledge?

These questions remind us of the age-old church question: How can we think that we, as unschooled individuals, possess the ability to understand higher spiritual values and know how to practice them religiously? Do we not need explanations and exhortations from preachers, priests, rabbis and gurus? Isn't there a narrow path? At least a dozen or so? And all standing in autonomy?

It seems the planetary rule is to go to the religious orders for spiritual guidance, not into some inner crevice of our being that may or may not be trustworthy. Might it not harbor dark thoughts and demands that could lead us to folly? Do we not need the steady hand of the civilizing church to rise above the animal in us all?

These devils most often appear as male sex urges, laced with alcohol and emboldened by greed and avarice. But perhaps these are ancient portraits of another age, and the churches are seemingly forbidden from updating any ideas of any kind at any time. We are rising above animalistic mind. But the churches still want to paint us as sinful wretches needing repentance. These painted pictures still scramble themselves before us like a Dorian Gray portrait today, the time-tarnished ways of controlling spiritualists by fear and mythology. But in my optimistic moments, I see that such degraded reasoning is fast disappearing.

The current thinking and seeking spiritualists are beginning to see fear and ordained hier-archies as a farce of epic proportions, a fraud perpetuated upon all of humankind to build power and wealth and, hopefully, obliterate all those opposed, those who did not see the true light, only another light, and did not share their earthly possessions with the organi-zation. Why, they ask, would we not support something deemed to be "God's house?" But who deemed it so , and does it make it so?

All of the religions have been guilty of slaughters, oppressions, even genocides. The time is fast dawning when spiritualists of the world will need their bloody history and stagnated dogma no longer, and will find personal guidance constantly from God's legions of teachers and guides working in the time-space mortal worlds.

Once we have established personal religion, a personal relationship with God, as the norm on the planet, we can proceed to reform or organize all-one-people supportive churches with activities that serve all the children of the planet, not just their fiefdoms.

In the coming age, those of us who learn to work directly with celestial guidance will be gratified with many blessings of the mind and heart, and we will be inspired to polish the evolutionary religions of the planet into the highest expressions that they can make.

The times when Jews and Christians and Muslims kill each other in war and send the horror and the financial burden to the good people of the world must come to an end. The people of the world will learn that divisive dogma is a worn-out tool of time and the new era of personal spirituality reaches out for all of this tiny planet's people. A new generation of leaders will emerge, who are aware of universe realities and are conscious servants to higher values.

In time, people will see that the various religious practices of this troubled world at this time most often represent radicalism, and that those who develop a personal relationship with God above and beyond manufactured dogmas, who communicate with the rest of this vast and well- connected universe of planets and beings via prayer and upreach are actually in the mainstream of cosmic spiritual thought.

How could fear have such a horrid grip upon our planet? Was it necessary at one time to teach humans reverence to God through fear, to help them rise above a state of savagery that we don't want to even imagine, including brutal destruction of other civilizations, slavery, even the sacrifice of their own children to assuage some bloodthirsty god.

The planetary history is there to see. Fear has dominated too often, and fear remains in power today. The great challenge of the age is to replace fear with love.

Universal Love is not being practiced on our planet; it is therefore being ruled by radical spiritualists, humans still polluted by the poisons of our animal evolution heritage, territorial, argumentative, self-serving, many even questioning the existence of God, many who blaspheme God's name for their own interests. Who are the religious radicals then, we or them?

The religions have marched and conquered with the armies of history, and they oppose each other still, and continue to amass their power against each other in any and all ways that humanity will tolerate. When can the people of this planet ever civilize their religions? When can they demand that they live up to their highest ideals, and even higher ones? Will this new age of 21st century spiritualists re-form and spiritualize these fear and control-driven institutions, at the same time that newer, fully altruistic religions are being formulated? These are indeed exciting times to both wonder and experience.

Those of us who now strive to work purely with celestial teachers sent by God will sometime be considered the unifying stream of living spiritual water on our planet. Religious organizations of true heart, mind and spirit will flow right into the ocean of God, a place where clear, sparkling water unites us all.

But ..... does my human viewpoint enjoy harmony with the wisdom of my mentor. He is Mantoube Melchizedek and I am one of his students. He is always available for counsel.

I would ask now if this is the correct mindset. As we have been in communication for some years, I wonder how many of these thoughts are inspired truth. I don't want to declare war on the dogmas but I do believe that when our views on spirituality are known, they will want to declare war on us. Can we avoid confrontations with the dogmas or is it inevitable and should we prepare to just refute them and stand up to forcefully state our case for personal religion?

Mantoube Melchizedek: What is possible is in your hands. This is your planet, and you have the head, the heart and the hands to drive it with your decisions. If confrontation is necessary, then do it by using the power of reason and the power of faith. It makes perfect sense that God would reside in spirit within each of his children, to pilot them and to experience their lives with them. If it does not make sense to some, then an open-hearted communication with God, the Universal Father, the First Source and Center, should solidify this new foundation of spiritual truth. We hope that you will move forward these higher truths and higher levels of faith, tolerance, respect and loving support that are so needed on your planet. Send people to God in the stillness and confidently let it be.

Are you saying that if large and critical numbers of people on the planet will turn to God and employ his guidance, then all will be well? I think this has become evident, but whether they will ever do so before the planet is either desecrated or even destroyed is still a question in most people's minds. Will we begin to care when it's too late? Will we care even then, if we can serve our own greedy self-interests?

by Jim Cleveland

MM: Mortal life, as you see, is a continuing stream of questions for you to seek to answer. Resist the temptation to ask me for answers, for they have often not been determined by the pace of time-space events, and the outworkings of vast numbers of free will decisions by unique mortals. We are excited to explore these questions ourselves, and observe the consequences, and the new possibilities that arise from these consequential acts.

Having prophets would be convenient to alleviate mankind's fearful dread of the future and what harms could be avoided, but such is not reality when the future is being constructed by all of you and each of you with huge numbers of free will decisions every moment. Humankind will come to see their free wills as perhaps the greatest of God's gifts, and will not take kindly to it being abrogated by governments, churches or profiteers. Increasingly, this is so. Thus, increasingly, the planet is quickening. Events are moving faster; mindsets are expanding; decisions are being influenced and altered; directions for actions are changing; clarified targets are emerging and more effective ways to hit those targets.

The world is changing more rapidly all the time and the pace of global knowledge expansion and spiritualization may well overcome the rapacious methods of our forefathers and their tenacious hold on power today. They define the key to power as Money and they seek to control it all; as they do, the basic health and nutrition needs of vast populations of people go unmet, and the poverty expands as the rich grow richer and their control near absolute.

The challenge of mankind is not to see the future, but to prepare for it, based on seeing a crystal clear picture of the planet's needs and how to achieve them. This includes a reformation of our societies that distributes the wealth according to productivity and not according to power, with enlightened governments that serve the people and not simply the bottom-line profits of the rich financiers who bought them into office. When your elected politicians are beholden to large donations of money, whose interests are they sure to protect? Are those interests the same ones as the people's, or do they engorge wealth and stockholder profits for the wealthy?

The real challenge to mankind in confronting and replacing corruption with institutions of true spiritual value is to do it as champions of higher spiritual values. Do it spiritually. Live with high spiritual values while confronting effectively the forces that impugn them or represent them poorly, hypocritically. Are you quite filled with this lecture?

I will only add that you will have more and less faith in much that you observe and many that you meet. The proverbial grain of salt is well applied.

True faith is best applied to God and Goodness, and all others in this mortal quagmire should be assumed to be struggling as you are, flawed and unpredictable. They can have advanced degrees and still be struggling, even more than a tramp on the street. They can be ministers of spiritual doctrine, and still struggling within, to separate the rote-like dogma

123

trap with enlightened inner thinking that would more strongly befit and serve a human of the 21st century.

The past can be a trap. The ancient past can be an absolute trap. The deeper one explores, the more one finds pits to absorb his time. Humankind could well devote more attention to the present and into the future, for many of the facts are in place today to predict the planet's future, and many of the needs to re-build our darker fates into an enlightened and illuminated future are ours for the application. The future largely belongs to the mortals of the planet.

Well, it seems to me that there is much being made of humans and celestial teachers working together right now, that much supernal help is coming, that we are entering a new age of clarified enlightenment, and that extraterrestrials are poised to come here in benevolence and service to help clean up our environmental messes. What are your comments about all of this supposedly imminent change...a sudden awakening, extraterrestrials showing up in a spaceship?

MM: I have not made it clear to you that you are in an evolutionary time-space world and you are each evolving within this framework. There is no future for me to predict. I have no prophecy and reflect only upon probabilities given courses of action underway. I reiterate that it is up to mortals to find answers, discover realities, evaluate options, make decisions, ask forgiveness, all those things that are involved in living the mortal life. The spiritual hierarchy does not, as a rule, intervene in evolutionary worlds that are working through their processes. We are not puppet masters and neither is God.

There is no contradiction in your receiving spiritual inspirations from us or any of God's legions and being masters of your own fate here. Spiritual inspiration has historically been available to mortal creatures as they come to the age of reason, as a child. There is this innate sense of right and wrong, and an inner spirit fragment of God that eternally urges the personality to goodness.

In present times, there is much speculation more direct intervention into your planetary affairs. Have you reached a pivotal point from which a new awakening will emerge? It is true that times of new awakenings come periodically on time-space worlds as the evolutionary beings increasingly disdain their animal origin natures to assume their true identities as spirit-indwelled children of the First Source. Learning that you are spirits with bodies, rather than vice versa, is a critical piece of knowledge that literally can transform civilizations when it is fully comprehended and put into action.

As you get into matters involving other planetary civilizations, you again press the envelope regarding what you should and must discover on your own and a piece of evolutionary knowledge that we might deliver unto you. It should be evident to the most knowledgeable beings on the planet at this point, you included, that the universe of planets is vast and the likelihood of living personalities on other worlds is overwhelming. Take this as your mandate to the future, the piece of wisdom you need to evaluate the reports now coming across the internet in all realms of research, investigation and speculation. This whole issue underlines the powerful of attraction of the time-space world experience, does it not? Discoveries are the excitements of your world, and when you learn to replace this higher excitement for the animal-like conflicts of evil and survival that now permeate your media, you will rise individually and collectively into a higher and more productive mindset. The glories of learning, exploring and achieving are straightforward and inspiring to light-driven voyagers.

I believe you're saying we should just wait and see how civilization evolves and do our individual parts with our own talents to represent spiritual values. But we can do frustratingly little when we see the horrors of corruption and warmongering, millions of starving children, wars and genocides, and hatred between creeds. It's hard to develop patience and exercise faith and calm in the face of things that we can't do anything about. Do you have any comforting words about that particular conundrum?

MM: It is okay to be restless to correct injustices and spread good will. This is what God wishes you to be in your mortal life. Be restless to find ways to serve goodness, truth and beauty. But quell your restlessness in faith that God's will cannot be abrogated; it will be done. Have faith in God and God's power and plans.

Many mortals will suffer horrible oppressions and ignoble deaths, but they are blessed by God. They will be served in glory in a higher life, and their opportunities will be bountiful. You cannot imagine the magnitude of angelic ministry that is attendant to your horrors, taking freed souls from their mortal suffering into a new light, and leaving accounts to be reckoned, for sure. Those who cause great suffering will have much retribution to pay. While you cannot see the justice that is administered in God's courts, rest assured that they are more reliable than your own, and that all is accountable and countable and not corrupted by the money worship that sullies all of your societies.

It is your evolutionary quest to work for your ideals, to educate yourself so that they are well-informed and that you can be productive in bringing the light of peace to all your fellows.

I would like to press you further on the matter of celestial help, however, and also help from beings from other planets. I don't necessarily understand this to be the same thing, I believe extraterrestrials may be spiritually-inspired beings, but I wouldn't equate their arrival here with a spiritual awakening of any kind. Would you? Should we look upon this apparently impending contact with other personalities an event of some spiritual magnitude or not?

MM: There are varying degrees of spiritual awareness and receptivity in the time-space worlds, of course. Those who have mastered the skills to visit here might be presumed to have a higher awareness of spiritual realities, simply by being attuned and conversant with the personalities of a number of other planets. Your isolation here does not serve you well. There are many worlds in God's domains of which you are yet unaware. The excitement is that we will be exploring them together, you mortals at your level of God's ascension plan, and me, the Melchizedeks and other cosmic citizens at their levels, and with the talents and knowledge they have to invest.

Those who are aware that the universe is, by and large, a friendly and benevolent place have much less foreboding about contact with other personalities. It is part of our learning to live in love, not fear, because of our faith and our realization that God's way makes perfect sense for each of us in our place within the universe plan. It is most likely that enlightened beings with the ability to reach you have realized and are practicing these spiritual service mandates. Of course, they are all yours for the discovery. There will be a milestone of amazement and excitement when the reality of space visitors and other worlds is so dramatically presented.

Well, some say the extraterrestrials are already here, governments are working with them even, foretelling their exposure, getting their technology secrets for their own gain, keeping the reality a secret, even as the evidence is piling up, even as more and more people have their own personal encounters. I think most of us just don't know what is real any more, and what is a cover-up of reality?

MM: Such is your plight, and your opportunity, on the time-space worlds. And I trust more will realize, as you apparently do, that we are not sources for the answers you must find or the experiences that you must have, your human bane, your human experience within your spiritual ascension plan. You see a growing body of evidence as to extraterrestrial contact; you simply must weigh the amount of evidence and its reliability, given the imperfect state of the human minds that produce the material you read. Living life is determining what is real. Living life determining the value of all things, and which ones to embrace and which to disdain. Your life is infinitely rich with moral decisions and each one can contribute to your soul growth, your worthiness to continue on God's ascension plan for you.

Perhaps you will consider that through history humankind has sullied many facts with embellishments, distorted many events to suit their tyrannies, lied blatantly to serve their ends at every turn. The corruptions that are inherent on your planet are so ingrained into the fabric of belief that the fabric itself must be cleansed. By this I mean the earth itself, its soil, water and air, and also the human institutions of education, religion and government, which have fallen to self-interest and the accumulation of wealth.

Too many want to become rich before they show loving charity, always promising themselves that they will. And yet their present lies follow in grabbing and taking and teaching their unfortunate offspring into doing the same. Loving charity is expected of all people by God, and more is expected of those who hold great wealth in the light of their neighbors' dire needs. When you transition from mortal life into the world of spirit, you will stand upon your record here and it determines how you will go forward. Perhaps rehabilitation is part of the process, that you will make amends and give service based upon how you have affected your mortal world. You will certainly find immediately that the lifeblood of the universe is service, cooperative building of civilizations, learning to work with many kinds of personalities, on your world and on others.

I know there is a divine plan, certainly. It's just a more immediate challenge here to make sense of events that are happening very fast, and quickening still, and with so many dangers. It seems we've embarked on an Age of Terrorism, in which everything that happens in the world is related to radical attacks. We have wars ongoing in two countries plus the usual middle east mess, and it appears more are going to be embroiled in it. Wars, driven by a few radical extremists, are draining our economies while massive human needs go unmet. The warmongering profiteers are altogether pleased to go to war. First we blow things up, then we pay to fix them. And lots of lives are lost and families shattered in the process. There needs to be a dynamic and immediate change here, but all the voices of reason are shuttled to the back pages while the self-serving bastards dominate world events.

MM: In your venting, you express your desire for higher values in your world. You are working for them and receiving spiritual guidance, as are many others. Patience will be required as planets move slowly in your frame of reference.

It would be advisable to find allies and work with them, not so much through a unity of doctrine, but through a unity of purpose, the bringing of the light and peace of good will to the planet. This can be achieved in many ways, in all the ways that each of you live your lives, in all the days that lie before you, and with all the opportunities for service that will appear to your face. Be aware, be caring, be loving. And move forward in faith. Celestial guidance will then be yours, surely and truly. You unleash the powers of the universe on your behalf with the purity of your intentions.

On another day, I started thinking again, and putting thoughts to paper.

The first step to becoming spiritual is releasing dogma. Through the centuries, humans have constructed religious institutions from their real and imagined understanding of documents written by fallible humans who are deemed to be infallible oracles.

The whole scenario is altogether human, and only related to true spiritual values in its parallel to the spiritual truths that can be gleaned directly from the human heart, in times of Stillness with God.

Church leaders are no more inspired or learned than you can be on the eternal values for they are simple and ingrained within you, within your indwelling spirit. Going to church can become ritual; staying at home and talking with God is a valid truth path to spirituality, if not religiosity. Churches all have some deleterious agendas they hide from general view, and which are not discussed openly.

Those houses of worship that center on God will survive and even prosper in the age of this new spirituality of connecting people directly with God. They will form and re-form themselves as to the perceived needs, wishes, interests and demands of the people in their flocks, and they will increasingly think for themselves and let themselves be heard in hallowed chambers only used to echoes. They will question the absoluteness of scripture, a confrontation long overdue, and they will find new ways to interpret scripture that will cleanse it of the distortions it has suffered at the hands of self-serving religionists. In truth, humankind has never been able to trust the integrity of those who translate scriptural texts, and those writings often have enough error and self- service in the original language, which is invariably controlled by the partisan power structures of the day.

Maybe I'm being too optimistic to see people rising up to take over their secular institutions, to spiritualize them above their corruptions with higher values, and to take over their dogmatic religions and insist that they reach out and work with God's children of all religions, and of all lands, to be worthy of support. Maybe I am; I feel that way when I'm feeling high about being God's child, and ultimately rising above all the turmoil down here.

Am I too optimistic? There are surely countervailing forces that may find a way to use fear in ever-bigger, ever-more dangerous ways to whip all of us into servitude, debt-ridden, weak and beholden servitude to pompous array of suited asses who revel in their richness and call it diving providence. The world seems to be at a critical juncture right now, with pressures of all kinds building.

What can you say to that? It seems maybe that my thoughts are somehow joined into the spiritual lessons that you would give me and so are reliable. On the other hand, taking dictation from you reads to me like a higher form of expression and it expands my thinking so ....

MANTOUBE MELCHIZEDEK: As the world shrinks, the problems seem larger. Everybody's problems will eventually become your very own, and you can see how the dumping of your problems on other peoples of the world is an evil you want to forsake and disdain. It is a small planet and you are all in it together.

The sum total of human knowledge is currently doubling in a matter of months and you need to find a way to utilize this potential progress in brilliant, interacting ways, and get the wisest among you into roles of leadership for these critical years that will effect your destiny. Find and work with dedicated spiritual seekers who are radical enough to proclaim their own personal relationship with God, their own confidence that they can remain open of mind and open of heart to all humankind regardless of their dogma or their culture.

I should say at this point that the dogma, or doctrines, of the organized evolutionary religions does often express high ideals and excellent spiritual knowledge, even some kind regard for unbelievers sometimes, but they are constructed to be inclusive of believers and exclusive of all who do not share the tenants, point by point and one by one. If a human would not do this, he would be condemned, even to a low-rent fire pit fate. It is possible to express high ideals on the one hand, and arbitrarily exclude many of God's children from sharing them on the other, unless they swear allegiance to manmade control edicts designed to keep the powers where they are. The one true path invariably betrays itself with its bias. There are as many paths to God as there are souls to walk them. That's an axiom you know.

I am altogether sure that we haven't convinced everyone that radical spirituality is being practiced by the churches, and that the "nefarious" channelers and transmitters have it right, talking to teachers who supposedly come from God. Should we then set about making a convincing case, and what is it, to your mind?

Channeling is by no means a foolproof exercise. Just as a pastor can misunderstand scripture and preach it that way, so too can persons remain engaged with their thinking mind while trying to transmit, and can send forth messages that are inaccurately weighted and can cause misunderstandings. To make a pure and fortuitous connection, you will do well to still your mind surely, open it into a wide and open plain of peace, and be fully separated from the voice that comes through. Submit unthinkingly, unwittingly, allowing your voice to blurt what it will.

It is not as much a task of trying as one of release, finding the center of worship, connect to it, and be an open page to what the celestials present with no analysis on your part at all. It is a flow, and coming from elsewhere than you, truly above and beyond.

Yet you can find truth from preachers or even people on the street if you are open to it. Each person has a unique vision of the world and their own solutions to its woes.

In all those unique, free will visions that you find today, there is already a deep inherent knowledge that spirituality and religion are personal, that God is personal to us, and that the churches either do the best they can, or they don't. It's not the critical thing. What is critical is how we live our lives, the growth of our soul into something of value, worth salvaging, worth saving, worth forgiving, worth supporting as we try to do better and the best we can. It's all personal. True religion is your personal relationship with God.

The concept of personal religion is more indelibly pressed into your society's fabric than you probably know. You can cultivate it, and when you send people to God in the Stillness, you've done a great service and surely the best that you can. If they go there with an open heart and mind, they will be rewarded. Many think they need to go to church; they perhaps really need to start talking to God, and, above all, take the time to listen, and learn. Why would you express your concerns and send your petitions, and not listen for a return? In some worlds, this would be considered rude.

I suppose you represent the vast universe of worlds, with which we'll hopefully have some time to interrelate. The current one, though, is in a total mess and getting worse. And it seems to me that we're not getting too far with solutions because we have so many points of departure or, in other words, we can't find a common starting point. Our dogmas and our nationalisms are sharp dividing lines to find that beginning point of working cohesively, globally, to solve our worst problems and quell the wars, which are all being fought for no good reason. Can you comment on all of that?

Your sentences strive for a starting point, as well. You have the answer in the Common Ground concept, rising above specific beliefs to revel together in our belief in God, and in Love as the embodiment of God, a God so rich that we can all experience God's expressions in unique and creative ways. There is a richness to life that puts one in a perpetual state of celebration when the vibrations of life are right.

In other words, each religion will have its olden scriptures which should logically be taken for the highest expressions of an ancient age, and not altogether trustworthy. The higher purpose is find higher expressions today, in the ways we live and love one another, in the ways we bring all of God's children together in our uniquely creative ways while we are here. There are many jobs where humans can do that.

The common goals of eliminating poverty and malice should be enough to unite all religions here. Why it has not done so is inexplicable to some of my colleagues, and they have perhaps not experienced the horrendous pressures exerted upon the human mind by a danger and deceit- laden sphere like yours.

If you will look around, you will see a great many of these global brotherhood initiatives taking roots around the world. It will become a burgeoning reality that humans want a better life and a better way of living it in the years ahead.

There are many battles ahead to win hearts and minds to a myriad of masked causes. If you would pull the veil back to reveal God and the spiritual hierarchy, they will become your allies in ferreting the false fulminations from the true inner core of your own spiritual essence. Once you make this deep contact, your strength will rise and rise some more, and you will become stronger, more able to express yourselves well, and more focused on the clarities of God and the simple, yet enobling, truths that you are to present to all people, regardless of their dogma. Their dogma doesn't matter, they do.

If they are persuaded to truly engage the Stillness practice, they will find a relationship of peace that will put their religious lives into true perspective. God and I matter. The churches work for both of us.

May I add in a sociological context that there is a lot of mythology in the organized religions. Yet, how much do you think it will matter if there is a new revelation, a powerful vision, a visitation from amazing other personalities of other worlds, strong spiritual energies that rise up from the indwelling spirits of humans into enlightened action projects that begin changing the world. There will come a time soon when these ancient scriptures will not be so revered or carry as much intellectual or theological weight as they do today.

The Bible says that when we mature we put away childish things. The amazing revelations of our times will increasingly mature us in our thinking, broaden our understandings and expand our knowledge of the universe. In time, many ancient scriptures will appear primitive, even quaint, the superstitious sometimes ruinous doctrines of bygone and very ignorant civilizations.

I think that's what we have today. Their corruptions are becoming so transparent. Are they becoming more transparent to other people as well?

I wish to say: Bingo!

I get it. And we can join the activist and reform movements of our choice and do as much as we can and will to improve the planet. That's the ticket, I think. Do good works. Is it an important work that we urge people to see that their religions are doing the radical things, and that direct mind communications with celestial teachers is not radical, and is, in fact, commonplace on most planets...that they've actually got it backwards in their minds?

Humans should really slow down on referring to "they" as some great amorphous power structure. It's always in ill-defined reference, though it's recently been related to a phrase, "politically correct," what most people think.

I assure you that most people will be wrong on many matters, and will invariably be wrong on spiritual matters. The infantile nature of your institutions seems only to perpetuate and expand the alienation that dominates your society. They become entities unto themselves, rather than a means for outreach and upreach into practicing the highest values.

It's certain that the vast needs of the people are transparent, to all except the purposefully blind. It is also certain that the need for cooperation, between all cultures, is implicitly visible to all of you. Taking steps to implement this truth seems very worthwhile work, and an integral pillar of your foundation.

If one's God would kill those who have a different idea of his identity, then the solution is radical and so is the God. This is not a logical idea about God, being representative of love and creativity on the one hand, and death and destruction on the other. Is this a two-faced God? Or a radical interpretation of God? I believe that God is all love, all the time.

If one starts with this point of departure, it is radical to think people who would kill one another in war for any religious reason at all. War does not represent God or any rational religion, only a radical one.

It is radical to think that God does not speak to each of us and in various ways if we seek his guidance. Some churches believe that God speaks through them, the houses of worship they have put up in his name. This is radical to think God organizes his human creations and has them reporting to other humans when God has the power to have an intimate connection with every child of his magnificent and bountiful creations in time and space.

It is radical to think that God would have a variety of designated stations from which to find his reality, when God's reality is in you and me, and everything we see. Churches of the new age would do well to organize themselves for all of God's children, not just those prescribing to a list of false doctrines that are prejudiced and biased against other kinds of people. These are poisons that have been injected into scripture for a very long time, and even today we are, of course, not without our vested interests who would twist all information to suit and serve their needs.

It is radical to think that God rewards true believers and punishes false believers, when God himself is responsible for the level of intelligence, and lack thereof, that is evidenced in all humans. God welcomes both those of brilliance and those of severe limitations, and all between, for the quality of mind is a factor of evolution.

It is radical to think that God is so cruel that he would devise eternal punishment, a fire of suffering without end, even to the most evil and misguided of his creations. I wonder, could anyone see Jesus doing such a thing? And can we not see Jesus' mission as strongly opposed to this kind of God-idol, one of anger and spite. That is a radical and highly contradictory way of looking at God, a two-faced entity who can provide supreme love and the ultimate cruelty. Woe be to the churchmen who put a second face of such ignominity upon God. I would not be anxious to serve their rehabilitation in the cosmic spheres.

It is radical to think that God wants sacrifices; what could you possibly have the he needs?

It is radical to think that health-damaging fasts and demonstrations of piety are serviceable to God, who would feel you could spend time in more productive service. And while the example of devoted faith is minimally laudable, that faith should soon find its way into genuine service, and not just a show of same.

It is radical to think that churches should establish a surcharge on your income, nudging themselves to the head of your financial obligations, even as you struggle with family needs. This is a usurpation of your God-given right to manage your resources for the greatest possible good. One's greatest needs are their families and neighborhoods and unless churches are going to service the full community with active service, it is likely that funds

132

should not be allocated to edifices with limited use. These are human decisions to be sure and in the future I believe they will be more enlightened, as people learn to support institutions of true Common Ground, of true and active service to all, and one that doesn't build fences according to judgmental doctrines.

It is radical for churches, which supposedly represent love, to stand by as nations go to war and send innocent soldiers to die horribly, and their families suffer. Any religion worth its credentials knows that no war is holy and no one should be killed in the name of any religious cause. It knows that wars squander resources that could feed and clothe the world and wants to do something about it.

And so you are radical people here, and your religions reflect it.

On the other hand, those who go into the Stillness and establish communion with God's spirits and your own indwelling spirit, then you will find that all fades away into the reality of the moment of deep truth, that you will live on despite these massive travails and tragedies, as the Spirit you have, having a unique and remarkable physical experience.

This is all remarkable too. But the churches will say that they already represent a sanctuary of sanity and spiritual peace in a world of turmoil, and they've been representing God to the best of their ability for a long time, and where would we be without them?

One should not rest upon one's laurels, especially if they haven't solved the vast problems of this troubled sphere. The good works they have done stand in the record but do nothing to advance the cause of Goodness going forward. Great needs are immediate. Without action, they are unmet.

Too many churches are guilty of burying and investing their resources into powerful money institutions where they are not put into service feeding and clothing and improving the dismal health conditions of the planet. They mask their great wealth behind a modicum façade of services.

Let them be. Quit worrying so much about what the religions are doing or not doing. They are the legitimate concern of those who are involved. Work within your sphere of influence, as all humans should seek to do. There is spiritual service to be provided in any work environment, for you are simply representing your highest beliefs in Goodness and Beauty and Truth. That is indeed religion. It is spirituality. It is your simple mission on earth, to bring forth these good tidings, in good faith that your Father God will lead you truly and to ultimate salvation after you have done your part here.

Godspeed.

Other works by *JIM CLEVELAND*
Books at www.authorhouse.com and bookstores worldwide.

NOVELS:

The Alien Intimacies
Philosophical
sci-fi adventure

Edge of Dark Light
sequel, suspense thriller
with extraterrestrials

Dark Riders
Suspense thriller
adventure

NEW SPIRITUALITY:

Beyond Cynicism
Liberating Voices
from the Spirit
Within

**The Celestial
Songbook**

**Celestials Over
Cincinnati**
Lessons of the
Planetary
Correcting Time

**Celestial
Songbook 2**

Jim Cleveland, a retired public relations and marketing executive, now lives in Mississippi.
He is a writer, poet, photographer, editor and spiritual activist whose projects and
networking interests are reflected in the
"Exploration of the Spiritual Universe" at www.lightandlife.com.